The Vibe-a-Thon™

creating your life from the inside out

Jeanmarie Paolillo

Vibe-a-Thon, LLC

www.vibeathon.com

Copyright © 2013 Jeanmarie Paolillo
All rights reserved

ISBN: 0615836860
ISBN-13: 9780615836867

Vibe-a-Thon is a trademark of Vibe-a-Thon, LLC

Tribe Vibe Testimony

"Praise and thanks for the Vibe-a-Thon! Though I have done meditation in the past and even found a semi regular practice, this experience of being led thru the process was and is remarkable. Jeanmarie's understanding of what to do and how, along with her down to earth language and writing skill allowed the process to seem simple. She gave me real life examples and offered clear instructions. Sure there is work to be done, sure I have to participate fully, but it's as though she's there in spirit leading me all the way. The book guided me through the tough parts and allowed me to take my own time digesting the material and feel fully supported at each place of pause. This is a plan, a book that I can continue to return to over and over again as I move along this path of discovery into my vibing practice. Thank you for this treasure." *Suzanne M.*

"As a lover of Jeanmarie, yoga, and self-help books, I was itching to read Vibe-A-Thon! But this is a self-help book like no other. Instead of trying to "fix" what so many of us think is "wrong" with ourselves, Jeanmarie encourages us to SHIFT the way we view the world and our lives. Jeanmarie's research, miraculous personal experiences, intelligence, and charming wit encourages the reader to believe anything she wants is not only possible, but absolutely will manifest when applying the Vibe-A-Thon technique. Vibe on!" *Claire B*

"The Vibe-a-Thon has been such an eye-opener. Going through the steps of vibing has taught me that I really can do anything I want with my life. It's not magic though--it's work--challenging work--but this book supplies the tools to help me accomplish the things I want. The truth is that this book overall just turned my world around. Bravo, JM. Thanks for a life-changer. Everyone I know is going to buy a copy. (I know a lot of people)." " *Liana R*

"Ever since I started doing the work from The Vibe-a-thon, my whole perception of life has been changing. I stress less on the things that I lack in my life or what I 'can't' have. I am more open to the possibilities of what life is offering me. This is not just limited on my subject I vibe on but all aspects of my life because vibing is not limiting. It is very much a holistic and opening experience. I am grateful for the tools Jeanmarie offered in her book that brought more mindfulness to my daily life and helped me change my habits that are no longer serving me. The book gave me the foundation needed by teaching tools such as a simple meditation technique but there was freedom to work individually and create my own piece of architecture that fits my lifestyle along with my needs and desires. I would highly recommend (and already have to many friends, family, and students) to dive into this new world of opportunity, The Vibe-a-thon." *Phoebe K*

"Jeanmarie truly is a humble expert. Not only does she lead and teach this idea of being mindful in her classes, but she's also a living example of what this kind of meditative awareness looks like in everyday life, which in NYC, is no easy task. This living example is how the Vibe-a-Thon was born." *Christy P*

"What the Vibe-a-thon offered me was a new understanding of fate, which is that it doesn't exit. I came away with the understanding that I am the only one responsible for my life and it's my job to create the life I want (spoiler alert: this also means there's no one to blame). Turns out that life is not a predetermined path that can be derailed by a series of "wrong" decisions. For me, the idea that there isn't a "right" or "wrong" way to go is so freeing. Finally the pressure is off and I'm more able to cultivate the life I want without the fear that I'm going to mess it up. There aren't mistakes, there's only navigating using the tools of meditation and mindfulness instead of a GPS. I now feel inspired to create and have so much gratitude for the fact that we get to decide what want." *Ashlee W*

"The process of "vibing" doesn't feel so much like a 28-day program but more like a gradual and purposeful shift in thinking and decision making. It's more like a set of tools to help you navigate the obstacles that arise in your life - I never felt like I was following a program but more like I was listening and responding to myself with a new sense of interest and engagement. It's not really "self-help", but more like having deliberate and decisive involvement in your own life." *Paula L*

For my Mom, who has always honored that I walk to the beat of a different drum;

And to those who showed me how to dance to the beat.

Table of Contents

"Destiny guides our fortunes more favorably than we could have expected. Look there, Sancho Panza, my friend, and see those thirty or so wild giants, with whom I intend to do battle and kill each and all of them, so with their stolen booty we can begin to enrich ourselves. This is noble, righteous warfare, for it is wonderfully useful to God to have such an evil race wiped from the face of the earth."

"What giants?" Asked Sancho Panza.

"The ones you can see over there," answered his master, "with the huge arms, some of which are very nearly two leagues long."

"Now look, your grace," said Sancho, "what you see over there aren't giants, but windmills, and what seems to be arms are just their sails, that go around in the wind and turn the millstone."

"Obviously," replied Don Quixote, "you don't know much about adventures."

~ Miguel de Cervantes Saavedra, *Don Quixote*

~Let the adventure begin~

Welcome to the Vibe-a-Thon!

What the heck is a Vibe-a-Thon? I admit, when the phrase came flying out of my mouth in conversation with a friend almost ten years ago, I was as perplexed as to what it was as you may be.

The first Vibe-a-Thon was self-imposed and self-created, a way for me to dedicate a specific period of time and supercharge my thoughts and emotions in line with something I was looking to bring into my life. Utilizing a consistent meditation practice to clear my mind—and practicing mindfulness in my daily life—as I continued to refine my vibe, I began to experience evidence of the vibe I was honing in my perception, contrast showing me what I didn't want so I could get clearer on what I did want, and opportunities to actively create what I desired in my life. It worked; it was fun and fascinating to explore exactly how my inner life (i.e., thoughts) impacted my external life.

During my first year teaching yoga full-time, I brought the Vibe-a-Thon to my students, to offer what I had created and see how it went in a group format. They loved it, and I was provided the opportunity to witness not only their experiences of creating wonderful things, but of opening up to the knowledge that anything and everything is possible when you learn to align yourself with what you want through the philosophy of yoga and through consistent practices of meditation and mindfulness, and then take appropriate action from that place.

Having grown up in the Roman Catholic tradition, I had always believed in the power of prayer and the potential for divine intervention, but generally in the form of a mild (or, sometimes, not so mild) bargaining tool. *If I do x for you, God, will you please give me y?* Sometimes it worked, sometimes not so much. And always it was contingent on some wonderful, scary, magical outside force that took my desire, judged it as worthy or not, and then granted manifestation based on those assessments. And yet, all the while, I witnessed people around me creating regardless of how they were living their lives. What seemed imperative for creating was whether or not they *believed to the point of knowing* they would get what they desired or, in equal measure, what they feared. Their ability to act as though that outcome was a foregone conclusion, along with the resultant emotional charge, seemed more important than anything.

I love the faith that I grew up with. The ritual of the Mass, the bible readings and the songs we sang (this was in the early seventies, when *Godspell* had leaked its musical magic into the mainstream and when Mass, for a brief and glorious time, seemed like a hippie Jesus rock concert). I signed on to all of it willingly for the most part. But God as separate from us, and in judgment of us, never made sense to me.

In my early days of high school, I experimented with pot and I remember being overcome by a feeling of peace and Oneness that I realize now I had been look- ing for through religion. Fortunately I was unwilling to commit myself fully to becoming a stoner, but the memory of those experiences stayed with me, nudging me in the direction of locating the core of that feeling.

I had my first—and extremely brief—introduction to yoga in 1979. I was a varsity cheerleader, and in spite of our lack of seriousness we received an invitation to a statewide competition. Before our big day, stress and nerves had gotten the better of us. Our coach asked the twelve of us to lie down on the ground and led us through what I now know as Savasana, the final resting pose in the physical practice within the yoga lineage. We closed our eyes, giggling and cracking jokes to mask the discomfort of basically not knowing what the heck was going to happen. Soon, the noise died down. As she led us into a deep state of relaxation, I found myself entering into the feeling that I had previously experienced in herb-induced states. But where before I felt disconnected, in this state I felt absolute integration, clarity, and peace.

The experience of Savasana stayed with me as I graduated high school, studied psychology at Indiana University, and made my way into the corporate world. I came to my study of yoga hesitantly, for it was the late eighties and yoga was not the booming, branded industry that it is today. I admit I had the same misconception about yoga that I still witness today: Is yoga a cult? Is it Religion? Isn't it Hinduism? Will I have to give up things in my life to do it? DO I HAVE TO CHANT OM?

Over my twenty plus years of studying both the physical practice of asana (poses) and the philosophy of yoga, I have come to a deeper understanding what it is really all about. Yoga is a way of life, providing us with tools we can use to create. It is an integral part of how the Vibe-a-Thon works, as you will soon understand.

What is yoga?

Yoga is a science, a way of life, and a philosophy that goes well beyond the ability to wrap oneself up like a pretzel or stand on one's head for long periods of time. The philosophy underlying yoga is thousands of years old. It is a scientific, nonreligious system that explores the nature of life and our individual place within it. It provides a practical approach to creating by understanding that all reality is perceived, and that individual perception is based on a myriad of factors, such as previous experiences and conditioning, conscious and subliminal thought patterns, and external environments. Understand the way you perceive life and the reasons why you perceive it as such, and you can work with the mind, change your perception, and create things anew in the world.

All reality is perceived. What does this mean? If we were to look at an optical illusion, chances are strong that I might see something that you don't see. Where I might perceive the outline of a vase, you might clearly perceive two profiles. A wall that looks brown to me may appear as deep, deep red to you. Where you may have a clearly defined conservative political view, I may be very liberal. We are products of the thoughts and mental impressions that have shaped us from our first breaths, and perhaps earlier.

The word *yoga* is defined as "to yoke" or "to combine," and the literal translation of yoga as a practice is *Yogas citta vrtti nirodha*, yoga as the cultivation of peace of mind. When we are in a state of peace in the mind we are at one with ourselves, free from the habitual patterns of thought that often lead us unknowingly away from the very things we strive for.

We can think of our true Self, higher Self, or Soul as a blank movie screen. On its own, a movie screen appears as a blank canvas. Thoughts are represented as the images projected onto the screen. The images do not *become* the screen, they are mere projections—and when the movie is over, the screen remains but the images have vanished.

We are the blank screens upon which the movie plays. Our work is to understand that the thoughts and impressions in the mind are simply projections.

We incorrectly identify ourselves as our thoughts in the same way that you watch a movie and get lost in the characters and the story line. Maybe you enjoy romantic comedies, or perhaps a good action movie gets you going. The manner in which you identify yourself by your thoughts is no different than buying a ticket to a movie. And by learning and understanding the work of the Vibe-a-Thon, you will discern what movie (thoughts, perceptions) will best serve you—and then learn how to create that movie.

The more mindful we become, not only in the moments of meditation or visualizing that which we desire, but in every moment of our thought-full life, the more clearly we can create the lives we are looking for. And here's the great news:

WE CONTROL OUR MINDS. THE MIND DOES NOT CONTROL US.

Once we understand that, we can begin to consciously examine the thought patterns that are running in our minds . . . to soften the *disallowing* thoughts that keep us away from what we want . . . and to mindfully cultivate those thoughts that will lead us in the right direction. This is the path, beautifully described in the Katha Upanishad:

> *Know the Self as lord of the chariot,*
>
> *The Body as the chariot itself,*
>
> *The discriminating intellect as charioteer,*
>
> *And the mind as reins.*
>
> *The senses, say the wise, are the horses;*
>
> *Selfish desires are the roads they travel.*

When the Self is confused with the body,

Mind, and senses, they point out, he seems

To enjoy pleasure and suffer sorrow.

When one lacks discrimination

And his mind is undisciplined, the senses

Run hither and thither like wild horses.

But they obey the rein like trained horses

When one has discrimination and has made

The mind one-pointed. (Katha Upanishad 3.3–3.7)[1]

The Upanishads is among the many texts related to the philosophy of yoga that we will explore through the course of the month. Another, Patanjali's Yoga Sutras, is one of the main philosophical texts in yoga, codifying the process of calming or stilling one's thoughts and coming to a place of Oneness—body, mind, and spirit. This collection of simple phrases, or sutras, illustrates both the path and practice of coming to a place of Oneness, a merging of the body, mind, and spirit into a unified Self. The Sutras have offered methods of clearing the mind and the path to peace for generations of practitioners over thousands of years.

If we create our reality by the quality of our thoughts, doesn't it make sense that by first calming our thoughts we learn to control them? Once we learn to control our thoughts, we can nurture those thoughts that will help us to create.

The path of yoga moves toward absolute Oneness within, away from the external things that keep us shackled to the physical world. So this begs the question:

---

1   Eknath Easwaran, *The Upanishads*, p. 88

Is it OK to have STUFF on the path of yoga?

Truly, one of the most interesting conundrums to practitioners of yoga is the relationship to *stuff*. We are an abundant society, and there is as much stuff to be had as any individual could possibly want. Is that a good thing? Is the pursuit of wealth in all its forms something to stay away from? If the goal of yoga is peace of mind and a life free from attachments, then is it wrong to want things?

No. Human beings are driven by desire. Even if there is a desire to have no desire . . . the desire needs to be there, to set the direction of our path. *Samkalpa* is our intention, or will and motivation. The mind is constantly in the pursuit of our intentions, making *samkalpa* the most important and time-consuming activity in our mind. Our thoughts are consistently centered on the things that we desire—whether it's our morning cup of coffee, the next thing on our to-do list, or a long-term goal. We create ourselves and our karma through these intentions, and *samkalpa* is the primary cause of our deeply held patterns of thought, word, or deed.

"Samkalpa is like a plan or strategy. We do something in a certain way to arrive at a certain goal. The result that we gain tells us the nature and the value of our action. No action is done without seeking some sort of result. This result depends upon the intention behind the action, not simply the externalities of what we do. Higher or spiritual actions seek a result that is not ego-bound, like the development of consciousness and the alleviation of suffering for all beings. Lower actions reflect ego desires—to get what we want; to accomplish, achieve or gain for ourselves in some way or another. Spiritual samkalpas direct us within and help liberate the soul. Ego-based samkalpas direct us without and bind us further to the external world."[2]

The path of yoga is not a path of destitution and limitation, as demonstrated through the four goals of yoga:

1. *Dharma*—Divine purpose, which we can think of as vocation. This refers to our status in life, our self-expression, and self-realization in preparation to be in service to others.

2. *Artha*—Prosperity, right possessions in life.

---

3. *Kama*—Enjoyment, including the joy or beauty of sensory experience.

4. *Moksha*—Liberation, freedom for full expression in life that comes through knowledge and experience.

We need to have things in order to maintain ourselves, to not be a burden to society, and to be in a place where we can be in service to others. So, create what you want your life to be. Be comfortable and fulfilled and well taken care of. And then, give all that you can to help others achieve what will satiate them.

Yoga is the science of spirituality. Moreover, there is compelling work in the greater field of scientific exploration that goes a long way in proving the philosophical concepts that constitute yoga.

Science that supports the path of yoga and vibing: quantum physics

> · *The most beautiful and profound emotion we can experience is the sensation of the mystical. It is the power of all true science.*

> *~ Albert Einstein*

There is a slight chance that as you just read the term *quantum physics*, your eyes started to cross or you went to the happy place that kept you safe during the plane geometry or advanced calculus classes of your youth. Not to fear! A brief understanding of what quantum physics is all about in the most practical terms supports both the philosophy of yoga and individual responsibility in creating.

Quantum physics can be thought of as the science of infinite possibility, and hints that we—as observers or participants—choose from these possibilities the actual events of our experience. Quantum physics flies in the face of traditional material science, which basically states that the primary source of causation is material interaction. In traditional science, life is defined through reason and proof—and what cannot be proven does not exist. In this view, consciousness is simply a brain phenomenon, a consequence of matter, and the case for a Higher Power, God, or Source of Origin is a challenge since it cannot be scientifically proven.

This idea of using pure reason to explain the world we live in (and our place therein) has been the mode of popular science for hundreds of years. And within the boundary of material interactions, there is no free will and little choice. This material science is ego-based and action-oriented. Interestingly, scientific evidence is never statistically 100 percent accurate. There is always some cause for doubt. So we, in fact, never really know what we think we know.

> *Ever since Descartes, philosophers in the West have been struggling to find a path to God and wholeness using pure reason.*
>
> *~ Dr. Amit Goswami*

Quantum physics, on the other hand, posits that consciousness is the ground of all being, and that we are all part of a Universal Consciousness that is popularly viewed as God. From this standpoint, consciousness chooses from quantum possibilities the events that make up personal experience.

Is there free will and choice from this view? In his book, *How Quantum Activism Can Save Civilization*, Dr. Amit Goswami states, "to the extent that we can access our higher consciousness and choose from there, you bet there is free will, complete freedom to choose from the quantum possibilities offered in any given situation. Free to choose the world as well as God and godliness, creativity as well as spiritual transformation."[3]

Many get caught up with the word *God*, as it may reference aspects of their individual conditioning that were challenging. In the many teacher trainings that I have led, the most interesting discussions surrounding the philosophy of yoga turn around the word God and students' associations with it. The following quote from Oprah Winfrey sums up the potential confusion nicely: "For all of you who get riled up when I mention God and want to know which God am I talking about, I'm talking about the same one you're talking about. I'm talking about the Alpha and the Omega, the Omniscient, the Omnipresent, the Ultimate Consciousness, the Source, the Force, the All of Everything There Is, the one and only God. That's what I'm talking about."[4]

---

3   Amit Goswami, *How Quantum Activism Can Save Civilization*, p. 52
4   The Oprah Winfrey Show, final episode, May 2011

If it feels better for you to call what is referenced above "Bobo," go for it. The name doesn't matter. What you experience as part of it does.

With quantum physics we find empirical evidence for the scientific approach to spirituality that is yoga. According to yogic philosophy, all reality is perceived. And perception is based in the mind. So we have infinite possibilities available to us, yet the mind limits what we can perceive in the same way that a horse's vision is contained by the blinders that are imposed on him. If my mind is limiting my perception, then the infinite well of possibilities seems unavailable to me.

What's a potentially-unlimited-but-currently-limited visionary to do?

We learn to vibe! Modern society has become quite skilled at *doing*, at making things happen through pure force and lots of action. What we have lost, and what I hope to help you regain, is the ability to *be*. To understand that creating in life has to be a combination of the ego-based, action-oriented, opportunity-taking YOU out in the world *and* the God-based, mindfully-present, intuitive, internally-seeking, vibing YOU.

It really is possible for you to create the life that you want for yourself. But it isn't as simple as "ask and it will come." There is no genie in a bottle. There is no magic. There is work to be done—and the work starts inside of you. The more you understand your own inner workings, the more you can direct your inner workings.

So let's look a bit at your inner workings, shall we?

From the outside in: Why is it so hard to create the lives we want?

Stress, AKA Our Lives on Slooooow Burn

The human being has evolved over millions of years. And yet, as we have transformed, grown, and developed over the millennia, a fundamental aspect from caveman days remains as part of our basic makeup. We are intrinsically hardwired for survival, with a system in place that will prompt us either to take flight or to enter into a fight at the drop of a hat. This sympathetic nervous system (SNS) is responsible for what was labeled "the fight-or-flight response" by Harvard physiologist Walter B. Cannon in the early 1900s. When in danger, the body processes hormones and takes significant action to get us out of the perilous situation.

Picture yourself thousands of years ago, strolling along the African savanna and minding your own business. Perhaps humming a lovely tune. Suddenly, you hear a mild growl behind you that you can't mistake for your own rumbling belly because you just ate. The roar becomes slightly more defined. You turn your head and see a large lion, whose belly is obviously not as full as yours. And he is looking—with absolute interest and what you can only interpret as longing—at you.

This is one of the very, very good reasons why the fight-or-flight response of the sympathetic nervous system evolved. What happens to get you out of the situation so that you don't become the lion's dinner?

— Blood surges to the muscles for hitting or fleeing

— Breath rate, heart rate, and blood pressure increase and the air passages of the lungs (bronchioles) dilate to better receive breath, so you can run faster

— Goose bumps make your hair stand up to make you look more intimidating to a potential attacker or predator

— Increased metabolic rate makes as much energy available to you as possible to get you the heck out of there

— Emotions intensify, getting your entire brain on board and ready for action

— Memory sharpens (so you can quickly remember, locate, run to, and climb the nearest tree)

— Body releases hormones—adrenaline and noradrenaline, or epinephrine and norepinephrine—to take care of all the above listed necessary processes to get you to safety. In addition, cortisol numbs pain and suppresses inflammation.

The following occurs as well when the sympathetic nervous system is activated:

- Digestion is impaired (Do you really need to waste energy processing food when that lion is licking his lips?)

- Sexual drive is impaired (see above)

OK . . . this all makes sense for you as the hopeful survivor in the savanna, right? What's interesting and important for us to understand is that this response is an ingrained part of our experience, and is invoked to a small—or not so small—degree *every time we are in a stressful situation*. The fight or flight effects listed above happen to a significant degree when we are in real strife or danger, but they happen as well when we deal with stressors in everyday life.

Let's face it. Life is stressful. Not that it hasn't always been—I don't know about you, but the idea of living during the time of the bubonic plague doesn't seem like a walk in the park to me. Stress is a part of life. And when we have the slow burn of a stressful life without employing any tools to rebalance our bodies and our lives, the long-term effects can be great:

- Gastrointestinal—ulcers, colitis, irritable bowel syndrome, diarrhea, constipation

- Immune—more frequent colds, flus, slower wound healing, greater vulnerability to serious infections

- Cardiovascular—hardening of arteries, heart attacks

- Endocrine—type 2 diabetes, premenstrual syndrome, erectile dysfunction, lower libido[5]

And the mental consequences are just as great. Anxiety, fatigue, and depression are some of the major effects that long-term stress has on the mind. In addition, when the sympathetic nervous system is aroused it stimulates the part of the brain that is hardwired to focus on negative information and to react

---

5   Licinio, Gold, and Wong 1995; Saposky 1998; Wolf 1995 cited in Rick Hanson, Buddha's Brain, p. 56

intensely to it. So feeling stressed sets you up nicely for both fear and anger. And when your emotions are ramped up, the rational part of your mind loses its ability to control the situation, turning you into some level of a hysterical, irrational mess. And much as a match lights a firecracker, the sympathetic nervous system, when aroused, affects the thinking part of your brain, the prefrontal cortex. It moves you further down the path of negativity. So you are out of control and reactive, unable to see things clearly and lashing out at the world. Not so good for creating.

We have evolved with a *negativity bias* that stems from our deep-rooted survival instinct. The brain is built more for avoiding than approaching—since it is the negative experiences that have generally had a greater impact on survival.

Wow. That's depressing, huh? Not necessarily! When we understand that we have a proclivity . . . a tendency . . . a leaning toward negativity, do we just throw up our hands and dig our hole in the mud? Of course we don't. When we understand how the body and the mind work we can take steps to balance the negativity and pessimism that keep us in limited perception. And that is the first move toward controlling the mind so we can direct it, and our lives, in the manner of our choosing.

To that end, we have the parasympathetic nervous system (PNS), the body's evolutionary antidote to the adrenaline-infused vigor of the SNS and fight-or-flight response. The PNS manages the normal resting state of your body, brain, and mind. It enables you to think clearly, quiet the mind, and foster tranquility. The more we can activate the PNS as part of our daily lives, the less control those normal stressors will have over us. And the less stress we have, the more clearly we can think. The more clearly we can think, the less reactive we become. The less reactive we become, the more *actively* we can create our lives, by moving away from the conditioning that kept us limited in the past.

Conditioning: Who are you?

We are individual human beings, but the texture and color and shape of our individuality is the sum total of our experiences. In the same manner that the food you eat creates the physical body you inhabit, the experiences and influences in your personal stratosphere shape your identity and, therefore, your life.

When we are conditioned, we no longer see possibilities as possibilities.

~ Dr. Amit Goswami

You are born into a family that identifies with a unique set of qualities and parameters. This includes your nationality and family identity. For example, a family with a strong ethnic lineage and background is going to look, act, and live differently than another family with a different background. All of the things that are considered a part of the heritage of the family collect to form you—from stories about ancestors, to holiday traditions, to the work ethic instilled by adults. Other factors that condition us to be the unique individuals we are include:

- The economic environment you were raised in

- The educational environment, including the attitudes about education within the family and peers

- The social environment—your friends (or lack thereof) and their influence on you

- The spiritual/religious environment (or lack thereof)

- The emotional environment (or lack thereof)

We are the product of conditioning, both conscious and subliminal, and the mind is built from the experiences we have. And so, when we talk about creating the life that we truly want for ourselves, we need to understand that there are self-imposed limits and boundaries on what we can actually do. Why? Because even though there is infinite possibility in life and we actually can be or do or have anything we want, we tend to *believe* only from within the confines of what we have previously experienced and therefore include in our realm of perception (i.e., things we "know"). There are so many possibilities that we never really give shape to because our conditioning keeps our field of perception and possibility limited.

On top of this, when we bring up a previous memory of past experience, it is often not a true representation of what that experience was. In discussing a shared experience with someone, we often realize that the memory they have is entirely different. The experience was a moment in time, and that memory—when brought up for review—is brushed and shadowed and highlighted with the remnants of your unique individual experiences. So it is always colored a little bit inaccurately, yet becomes a stronger variable in your conditioning with each revisit. The same thing is true for your friend's recollection. And both you and your friend take that inaccurate memory of something long gone as evidence—usually against making a change in your life.

We are thinking for the vast majority of our lives, but it's not even directed or focused thought! Most of the activity of the mind is undisciplined thought associated with memories. Some memories are conscious recollections of specific events or information. Others are the residue of past experiences that remain under the radar for the most part, but can take a strong role in shaping the inner landscape and atmosphere of the mind. This can help to explain why we may consciously try to create something in our lives but it never seems to come to fruition. On the surface, thoughts are going in the right direction. But underneath is another story.

There's something you would like to create in your life, and when you first think of it, it feels wonderful and fun and exciting. It's a great idea that often gets squashed like a bug from the weight of your past experiences.

Previously, you learned about the idea of a true, higher Self and how our thoughts cloud that. Moving deeper into this exploration of yogic philosophy, we learn that a recurring pattern of thought, word, or deed is known as a *samskara*.

When a kerosene lantern is first lit, the glass is clear and the light of the flame is visible from the center. As more of the fuel is burned, fumes begin to cloud the glass. Over time, if the lamp is not attended to and cleaned, the glass can become so fully coated with the residue of the kerosene that the flame is no longer discernible. It's as though the lamp has walls made of lead, not glass. And yet the flame continues to shine just as brightly from within. We just are not able to see it.

It is the same thing with the mind. The real you is unaffected, undisturbed, pure light and peace, open to infinite possibility. Thoughts and impressions, including the effect of the experiences in your life, are similar to the first clouds of kerosene that start to fog up the glass. When those thoughts become habit or thought patterns and tendencies, those *samskaras* cover the glass even more. Further, when *samskaras* become ingrained, they become deeply held parts of our personality. In yoga, we call these the obstacles, or *klesas*. The five *klesas* traditionally listed are ignorance, ego, desire, aversion, and fear.

If we are so obstructed by our thoughts, how can we hold the vision of what we want to create? The truth is . . . we can't! Those *samskaras* will limit us to the confines of what we "know" (and, potentially, don't want) and away from what we do want. Because you can talk about what you want until you are blue in the face, but if you don't truly believe that what you are looking to vibe on is possible and deserved and viable, then not having what you want is what you really perceive as your reality. **And what you perceive you receive.**

Beliefs are thoughts both deeply rooted and reinforced, like a path created through the woods over time. And the more our thoughts are in line with our beliefs, the more our minds are set up to find evidence in the world in support of our beliefs. Why? Simply put, our thoughts are in line with certain perceptions, and it is the work of the ego to look for validation of our perceptions.

You are the pure light burning within the kerosene lamp. You are the blank movie screen, upon which impressions are made. If you identify yourself as the impressions in the same way that you get caught up in the action or romance of the movie on a screen, you lose the power to shape your thoughts objectively and create your life. But when you learn how to experience yourself as witness to the thoughts, how to become less reactive to the thoughts so that you can open to your true field of perception (which is infinite) and then actively create thoughts and beliefs in line with what you want—well then, the world is yours for the taking. By internally conditioning your mind through meditation and mindfulness, you can lessen the effects of all the external conditioning that keeps you from what you want. As the mind opens up, it can begin to perceive evidence that what you are looking to create is at first possible, and then probable. You come to see the not-so-great stuff or *contrast* as nothing more than showing you what you don't want in order to get clarity on what you do want. Through mindful navigation, opportunities to actively create come. And then you are on the path of actively creating.

Let's look a little bit more at how the mind works.

Your brain: What the heck is in there and how does it work?

The brain is the center of the nervous system and a highly complex organ. It has been estimated to contain 50–100 billion neurons, the basic building blocks of the nervous system. Neurons are cells that pass signals to each other via as many as 1000 _trillion_ junctions, known as synaptic connections.

The gray matter of the brain is largely composed of the cell bodies of neurons. And they are all there, at the ready to forge new synapses in the form of patterns of thought for us to create what we want—to get away from the limiting _samskaras_ and _klesas_ mentioned previously and to create new pathways that are consistent with what we want the mind to perceive, so that we can then create it.

In principle, the number of possible combinations of 100 billion neurons firing or not is approximately 10 to the millionth power, or 1 followed by a million zeros. To put this quantity in perspective, the number of atoms in the universe is estimated to be "only" about 10 to the eightieth power.[6]

An understanding of the two hemispheres of the cerebral cortex—known commonly as the left and right brain—helps to explain the process of vibing. Though each hemisphere is unique in the types of information it processes, they communicate with one another and work together to create a seamless perception of the world. We can think simply of the left brain as the ego-based side focused on "doing," the right brain as the more intuitive "being."

The left hemisphere is the home of the ego center, providing an internal awareness of the things you identify as yourself. It is the part of the brain that processes language and thinks in patterned responses to incoming stimulation. So it's the part of the brain that can very easily react based on what has been previously experienced. Over time, it can establish neurological circuits that run relatively automatically, thereby creating both _samskaras_ and _klesas_. The left brain is detail-oriented, analytical (and judgmental), rational, sequential, and can process large amounts of information quickly.

---

6   Rick Hanson, _Buddha's Brain_, p. 15

Because of its ability to process language, the left hemisphere is the storyteller, and the space where brain chatter can fill up and cause all kinds of chaos. This capability is designed to make sense of the world outside of us, functioning by taking whatever details it has to work with and weaving them together in the form of a story. It can also be either highly effective or inept when it comes to creating the lives that we want, depending on how we manage the chatter and stories. When we are not in a place of understanding the mind and actively shaping how we think, the thought patterns that loop and the stories the mind tells keep us in a place that is not in line with what we want. But when we learn how to clear the clutter in the mind and bring in thoughts that reinforce what we are looking to create . . . then we have the keys to the kingdom.

In her brilliant work *My Stroke of Insight*, Jill Bolte Taylor describes her experience of having a stroke. A neuroanatomist, she was able to witness the effect a severe stroke to the left hemisphere of the brain had on her as the stroke was happening. The following passage gives great understanding about the right hemisphere of the brain, which she experienced in its totality due to the trauma to the left hemisphere: "I remember the first day of the stroke with terrific bitter-sweetness. In the absence of the normal functioning of my left orientation association area, my perception of my physical boundaries was no longer limited to where my skin met air. I felt like a genie liberated from its bottle. The energy of my spirit seemed to flow like a great whale gliding through a sea of silent euphoria. Finer than the finest of pleasures we can experience as physical beings, this absence of physical boundary was one of glorious bliss. As my consciousness dwelled in a flow of sweet tranquility, it was obvious to me that I would never be able to squeeze the enormousness of my spirit back inside this tiny cellular matrix."[7]

The right hemisphere of the brain is the visual-spatial hemisphere. It is more "big picture" than the left hemisphere, and is considered the more creative part of the brain. It is sensitive to nonverbal communication, is intuitive and can decode emotion, is content, compassionate, optimistic, and nurturing. It is open to possibilities and can think outside the box, and is therefore the more adventurous side that can open us to something new. It is able to be in the present moment, and is the place we come to when the chatter of the left brain has calmed down and we feel a sense of peace and rightness with the world.

---

7   Jill Bolte Taylor, *My Stroke of Insight*, p. 70

Using the left and right hemispheres of the brain effectively is where the true work of vibing stems from. We need to open up to the infinite possibilities and creativity offered in the right hemisphere, and then train the thought patterns in the left hemisphere so that the two of them are in sync with what we want. And then, as we bring the mind to this new place, our perceptions change. As our perceptions change, the mind looks for (and finds) more and more evidence in support of the vision—and contrast that more specifically elucidates the vision, which allows us to further clarify what we want. From there, appropriate opportunities to actively create present themselves.

> *The challenge is simple: we are not what our genes are; the body is. We are what we think. Conditioned behavior may be dictated by our genetic makeup, but when we get below the surface level of consciousness and get hold of the thinking process itself, we can go beyond conditioning and actively create—and change—our lives completely.*
>
> ~ Dr. Amit Goswami

Right on!

We are dynamic beings. Our cells are constantly changing, and our organs are therefore constantly changing as well. The brain is a highly dynamic organ, though this was not always understood. For hundreds of years, mainstream medicine and science believed that brain anatomy was fixed. That "after childhood, the brain changed only when it began the long process of decline; that when brain cells failed to develop properly, or were injured, or died, they could not be replaced. Nor could the brain ever alter its structure and find a new way to function if part of it was damaged."[8]

In *The Brain That Changes Itself*, Dr. Norman Doidge demonstrates through fascinating case studies the ability of the brain to—as the title adeptly describes—change itself: "I began a series of travels, and in the process I met with a band of brilliant scientists, at the frontiers of brain science, who had, in the late 1960s or early 1970s, made a series of unexpected discoveries. They showed that the brain changed its very structure with each different activity it performed, per-

---

8   Norman Doidge, *The Brain That Changes Itself*, p. 9

fecting its circuits so it was better suited to the task at hand. If certain "parts" failed, then other parts could sometimes take over. The machine metaphor of the brain as an organ with specialized parts could not fully account for changes the scientists were seeing. They began to call this fundamental brain property *neuroplasticity*."[9]

We have all heard examples of people triumphing over disastrous conditions and tremendous odds. And we are no different! As you come through the process of the Vibe-a-Thon, you will begin to see that you can change your thoughts to change your perceptions so that they are in line with the life you wish to create. And then you will be able to take action from that place to actively create.

You are now undoubtedly both excited and daunted by the prospect of working with the mind. How exactly do we do that?

The beauty and necessity of meditation

I will admit to you, when I first started playing around with meditation approximately ten years ago, I thought it was awesome. And the reason why I thought it was awesome was because I would close my eyes and allow myself to daydream for whatever period of time I had chosen. Good thoughts, bad thoughts—they ran amuck until I opened my eyes again.

I was fortunate to have my first real teaching and understanding of meditation with Sharon Salzberg during a monthlong workshop. It was then that I made my first attempts at not following the incessant racket, at coming back to my predetermined point of focus over and over again. I would reach a stage where I felt that I had gotten "there" only to find myself a moment later either immersed in yet another daydream or fully ensconced in a memory. (I remember well a day when I spent the entire time sitting in meditation and trying in vain to get away from the song "Me and Mrs. Jones.")

Finally, many years later, I have come to understand that there is no right or wrong in the practice of meditation. There is only the practice . . . and the process.

9   Ibid., p. 11

Meditation is clearing and redefining the clutter in the mind. Imagine that you would like to redesign one of the rooms in your house, but it is filled with lots of stuff—so much stuff that you can't get a clear sense of the amount of space available, how the light plays in the room, how you would like to rework the things you own in the space, and what new objects you might like to bring in. The first thing you need to do is to clear the room out entirely, and then to put back into the space the furniture and pictures and such that are in line with how you would like the room to look.

Through the process of meditation, we focus our attention away from the chatter, and thereby clear out the clutter. As the mind gets more calm and focused, we are able to witness the thought patterns that are keeping us out of sync with what we are looking to create. In sitting with those *samskaras*, we are able to understand that they have no hold over us and to let them go. In doing so, our field of perception becomes clearer. Once the space is clearer, we can bring in the thoughts that support what we are in the process of vibing on.

I am passionate about the practice of meditation because 1) it works; 2) it is the best way I have found to become less reactive (and therefore, more active) in both my internal and external lives; and 3) it is tremendously good for us on all levels of life. Take a look at some of the benefits of regularly practiced meditation:

Benefits of Regularly Practiced Meditation[10]

- Increases the gray matter in the brain

- Improves physiological functions associated with the gray matter in the brain including attention, compassion, and empathy

- Increases activation of left frontal regions, which lifts mood

- Increases the power and reach of fast, gamma-range brain waves in experienced practitioners

- Decreases stress-related cortisol

---

10   Herbert Benson, *The Relaxation Response*, p.xli

- Strengthens the immune system

- Helps a variety of medical conditions, including:

    o   Cardiovascular disease

    o   Asthma

    o   Type 2 diabetes

    o   Premenstrual syndrome

    o   Chronic pain

- Other conditions that, to the extent caused or affected by mind/body connections (such as stress or fight-or-flight response), can be significantly improved or even cured when self-care techniques are employed:

    o   Angina pectoris

    o   Cardiac arrhythmias

    o   Allergic skin reactions

    o   Anxiety

    o   Mild and moderate depression

    o   Bronchial asthma

    o   Herpes simplex (cold sores)

    o   Cough

    o   Constipation

    o   Diabetes mellitus

- o   Duodenal ulcers

- o   Dizziness

- o   Fatigue

- o   Hypertension

- o   Infertility

- o   Insomnia

- o   Nausea and vomiting during pregnancy

- o   Nervousness

- o   Many forms of pain: backaches; headaches; abdominal pain; muscle pain; joint aches; postoperative pain; neck, arm, and leg pain

- o   Postoperative swelling

- o   Rheumatoid arthritis

- o   Side effects of cancer treatment

- o   Side effects of AIDS treatment

- Helps address numerous psychological conditions, including:

- o   Insomnia

- o   Anxiety

- o   Phobias

- o   Eating disorders

The practice of meditation and/or contemplation is as old as civilization. It is the exploration of every spiritual and religious teaching, each with a particular path but all leading up to the same place of Oneness with all things, and to ultimate union with that which is larger than us all, that which we are all a part of.

When you make the two one

And when you make the inner as the outer

And the outer as the inner,

And the above as the below,

And when you make

The male and the female into a single one

So that the male will not be male

And the female not be female

Then you shall enter the kingdom

~ The Gospel of Thomas

Focusing your attention through the process of meditation is where you train the mind. That is the first step, for the true culmination of vibing occurs when we continue the cultivation of clarity that begins in meditation and combine it with practicing mindfulness in daily life. This is possibly the most powerful and compelling way to shape the patterns of the mind. In this way, we can resculpt our perceptions, disengage from previous conditioning, and change our lives.

How the Vibe-a-Thon works

The Vibe-a-Thon works best if followed over the course of a month or over a longer period of time, depending on individual needs. The first day of each week has a longer chapter, each describing a certain aspect of the process and including exercises for you to complete. On the following days of the week, you will read a shorter piece to keep the inspiration and the vibe up. These shorter pieces will bring you to a further understanding of the different points described in this introduction, and will offer contemplative exercises to help you stay with the process.

Supplemental information, support and community for vibers can be found online at www.vibeathon.com.

A final thought

My hope for this book is to help you see that you truly can have or be or do anything in your life, but it takes work. And the work is glorious.

I hope to introduce as many people as possible to the philosophy of yoga and to demystify its mystical misinterpretation. And to help you start on the path of clearing the clutter in your mind through meditation and mindfulness, for that is truly where we direct our lives away from a habitual, reactive stance and toward an active experience of creating.

I hope to show that creating your life is not only rewarding, but can open you up to see that there is no bad, there is no ugly. There is only evidence in support of what we are looking to create, and the contrast of what we don't want to help further define what we do want, leading to opportunities to actively create.

Mostly, I hope that you are successful in creating what you want, and that it is amazing. Because you are amazing, life is amazing, and the possibilities are truly infinite.

Ready? OK, then let's begin!

Week One

Do you believe in miracles?

I know it's a corny question. But anyway . . . do you?

I recently came across a documentary on the 1980 US Olympic hockey team (USA vs USSR). At that time, I was a junior in high school. And I couldn't have cared less about hockey as a sport, but let me tell you—it was a magical event. A group of American college kids up against the best hockey team in the entire world. There was a lot of tension between the two countries and it seemed to represent more than just a game. As I watched the documentary, I got goose bumps.

I think we are all a bit like that hockey team. Or any other underdog in the history of mankind who ever displayed the audacity to believe they could have what they wanted in life.

You know how great it feels when you watch a movie or hear a story like that? Do you know why it feels so great? Because it touches that space deep inside each one of us—our Source, our Soul or true Self—that knows how unlimited the possibilities are. The part that knows that we can create whatever it is that we want, without limit or hesitation. Unfortunately, the part that knows all things are possible is covered by the compilation of limiting thoughts and impressions that make up the mind. We need to open the space in the mind to possibility, and to work with the quality of our thoughts so that we come to a place of belief that is in line with what we want. And so we need to shape the mind's ability to perceive evidence that validates that we are on the right path, to discern contrast highlighting what we don't want and use it to clarify what we do want, and take the newly perceived opportunities that will bring us toward what we are looking to create.

Think about it. Why is it that we feel as though we have to struggle and suffer and plod along to create the wonderful, well-deserved things we want out of life? Why do we hold on to the belief that life is hard and then you die and enter either into vast nothingness or into heaven (but *only* on the condition that you suffer and struggle and eat your peas and work, work, work while you're here)?

What if that's *not* the case? What if, in fact, the purpose for us in life is to enjoy and play and imagine and create wonderful experiences and things? What if life is meant for the purpose of joyful creative expression here on earth?

I know that this goes against the grain of some belief systems out there. But the thing that has become profoundly interesting to me is this: *Who actually knows?* Can anyone prove either theory? Is it a fact that we live to suffer and then die, or live to joyfully create? And even if neither theory can be proven, wouldn't it be nicer to live in the second state of joyful creation?

There are things that you would like to develop in your life. We all have these desires, but most of us either live behind the perceived limitations of our ability to get what we want, believe our desires are unachievable, or can't quite figure out just how to reach the target. We struggle to come up with some way to *make it happen*, and get entirely caught up in the action.

And therein lies the problem, because it's not solely about the action! It never is. Before taking action in the world, we need to be clear about what we want to create. The inner exploration is as important and necessary as the outer work. And the inner exploration means looking consciously at the actual thoughts, beliefs, and emotions tied to the desire. Once you start to undergo the process of clearing your mind through the practice of meditation, and to mindfully engage thoughts that are in line with your inspiration in everyday life, you will begin to perceive more evidence of and opportunity for the experience of what you desire. Because the mind is highly refined in its ability to hone in on what we are conditioned to look for, deep within its structure.

Look at those people in life who have created something. There are a million examples to choose from, but each story has a common denominator. At a very deep level, those creators not only desired, but they believed in the inevitability of their creation with every fiber of their being. This belief kept them focused singularly on what they wanted, no matter what anyone else said or did. They opened their minds to the point where they could see the possibility. And in seeing the possibility, they were able to perceive evidence of what they were looking for, evidence that pointed them in the right direction. Their thoughts about what they wanted were strong and clear enough to create a belief that it was possible, leading to an emotion of surety in its inevitability, and the patient conviction that it would happen in its time. When conflicting evidence (contrast) presented itself, they were able to view that evidence objectively and to use it to more fully define what they wanted to create. From that state they were able to take advantage of opportunities to actively create. They were in sync.

They were, in effect, vibing and on their way.

We've all had moments in life when we knew something was going to happen. And whether that thing was seen as positive or negative, in the second it happened chances are there wasn't much shock or surprise at the actual event (although we may have been shocked at how easily or smoothly or quickly or catastrophically it happened). The occurrence was our subconscious vibrational alignment with what we were expecting, because we create our own reality. We really do. And we can create it within the confines of the beliefs and conditioning that we have held during the years of our existence or we can open ourselves up to an understanding that we can expand our minds and our lives in the exact ways that we dream of. To fully know that there is nothing beyond our grasp unless we deem it so.

Here is where the science of spirituality that is yoga can help us greatly. In the introduction, the four goals of yoga were listed, describing the path not as one of limitation, but as one of understanding the difference between need and want. It is a path of abundance for ourselves—so that we needn't be a burden to others and, more important, so that we are able to live our lives in service to others through *dharma* (vocation, purpose), *artha* (prosperity), *kama* (enjoyment), and *moksha* (liberation).

Isn't that cool? We can have the lives we want. And all we have to do is follow these simple guidelines:

Number 1: Decide on what you want!

> *Ask, and it shall be given to you; seek, and ye shall find; knock, and it shall be opened unto you: For everyone that asketh receiveth; and he that seeketh findeth; and to him that knocketh it shall be opened.*

> *~ Matthew 7:7*

The science of quantum physics asserts that there is an infinite field of possibility. And this field is available to everyone, but only to the extent that our minds are open to it. In the same way we are all extensions of this infinite field, and our work is to line the mind up with this energy in order to create what we want. Because it's all there for the creating, with both unlimited possibility and resources available once we expand our perception to see it.

It can be challenging to figure out what we actually want. And often, something that we are reaching for externally is nothing more than a physical representation of what we are really seeking internally. Material wealth is greatly valued in today's society, but what about internal wealth? Instead of looking for more money, perhaps you will find what you are looking for by opening up to security within. If you are looking for a relationship, maybe the work of the Vibe-a-Thon will be to open your heart up to the experience of love in all its forms. This will go a long way to expand your field of perception, leading you toward opportunities to create and experience that which you seek.

It's vital to understand that this isn't a genie in a bottle. It's not as simple as asking for something consciously and waiting for it to appear as if by magic. You can consciously want something, but your *samskaras* (deeply held patterns of thought, word, and deed) and *klesas* (ingrained limitations in the personality) need to be cleared up and softened as well, in effect releasing the unseen shackle holding your dreams at bay. We can accomplish this in two ways: through the practice of meditation and through mindfulness in our daily lives. Until we train ourselves otherwise, we spend most of our day in unfocused thought! The more we take on the work of both controlling and directing our thoughts, the more the field of perception will open to us. Which brings us to the second guideline . . .

Number 2: You have to line up with your aspiration vibrationally.

All reality is perceived. And perception is based on conscious thoughts, past experiences, conditioning, and other subliminal impressions in the mind. Once we have figured out what we want, we need to change the myriad of mental impressions responsible for our perception, so that our thoughts, beliefs, and emotions are in sync with—not fighting against—what we want.

You have to be *lined up* with the thing you desire. In other words, you have to be in a state of openness to the infinite possibilities (which include what you desire); you have to believe that achieving your desire is not only possible, but that you are truly on your way; then your field of perception can open up to show you evidence that you're on track and opportunity leading you step by step toward the easeful creation of what you want. Because when we are vibing there is no struggle!

If you desire more money, but are complaining that you don't have enough, you are not lined up with "more money" because the focus is on your lack of money. In this case, you are actually going to perceive more evidence of your lack of money because *what you perceive you receive*. You are a *vibrational match* to lack of money.

If you are not in a great place with your health and want to feel better, but continue to focus on the illness and on why you're not well, then you are vibing on illness, not on wellness. You are, in fact, perceiving and receiving more of the not-feeling-great state because your mind is set to find more experience of illness. Yikes!

Research shows that evidence that supports the way you see the world sticks to you like Velcro and anything that disproves your worldview is repelled as if off Teflon. In one study, participants read an article that described research on the harmful effects of smoking and that also noted some faults of the study. Although the article contained an equal number of points about the harmful effects of smoking as it did about faults of the study, the smokers were more able to recall the study flaws, whereas the non-smokers were more able to recall the dangers of smoking. Further, given the opportunity to read more information on a topic, people will choose documentation that supports the belief they already hold[11]. We are wired to seek out evidence that validates our belief.

An interesting conversation I had with someone during the first Vibe-a-Thon describes the confusion on this point. She wanted a relationship, but felt both downtrodden and absorbed in the potential of a future alone. When I explained that she needed to get herself lined up with what it would feel like to already

---

11   Baumeister RF Bratslavsky E Finkenauer C and Vohs K D (2001). Bad is stronger than good. *Review of General Psychology,* 5, 323-370.

have the love she craved in her life, she looked at me quite cynically. Our conversation went something like this:

> HER: Well, I keep on vibing on love and looking around for it, but nothing is happening. I've asked and I've asked and I've asked and I'm getting nothing.

> ME: It makes sense that you feel you're getting nothing. Because what you're looking at is the fact that you have nothing. And if your thoughts are predominantly about having nothing, then that's what you will perceive. And what you perceive you receive. So if you're focused on the fact that you have nothing, your mind is set to seek out more evidence that you have nothing. And then, you'll get more of nothing.

> HER: But if there's infinite possibility for everyone, then why is it taking so long for me to get what I am looking to create? Why should it be so hard for me and so easy for all of my friends?

> ME: Look at what you just said. You may say that you are lined up vibrationally with what you want, but your statement shows that you're actually lined up with the perception that it's hard for you and easy for everyone else. Your perception is totally lined up with "finding a relationship is hard and takes a long time," and so that is what you're going to continue to get! You have to get your vibe up, through your thoughts and feelings as well as through the action you take.

Let's say you're listening to 630 AM on the radio but you want to hear what's being played on 93 FM. Would you keep the dial on 630 AM and demand to hear what's being played on the other station? Of course not. And it's the same thing with your vibration. You can't get to the good stuff that really is available to you if you're focused on what you don't have. You've got to shift your perception and your vibration. You've got to be a match. When you have opened your mind so that your thoughts and emotions are in line with what you desire, you will begin to perceive evidence out in the world that validates that you are on the right path. At first, these may be little bits that don't seem like much—maybe more like small coincidences. You'll see contrast as a useful tool in further clarifying what you are looking to create. In addition, when the blinders that limit your field of perception begin to peel back, opportunities for actively creating or manifesting will begin to present. Again, these may seem infinitesimal in the scope of what you're looking to create, but this is how the path of creation unfolds. When we stay mindful and continue to actively hone our vibe, from the opportunity we perceive further evidence and contrast . . . from there we come upon more opportunity . . . and so on and so on.

Nobody is responsible for your life except you. When we can't manifest what we want, it's because the vibe about it isn't clear. There are divergent thought patterns clouding the spark inside that is ready to create. And until we learn to control the thoughts and direct them, all that is being sent out by you (and re-flected back to you) are the scattered thoughts. The more you work to line up your thoughts—and eventually your emotions and your perceptions with what you want, the more easefully you will start to see evidence of and opportunity for that thing or experience. You have to take responsibility for the energy you bring to your vision, and to your life!

We all have beliefs. Beliefs that we were brought up with, ones that we ab-sorbed from the people around us and from the societies in which we live . . . and those that we create within ourselves from the experiences and situations of our lives, both good and bad.

But what is a belief? A belief is simply a thought, replayed over and over again, until it becomes a *seemingly* concretized part of our being.

> *Whatever you might hope to find, among the thoughts that cloud your mind . . . there won't be many that ever really matter.*
>
> *~ Jackson Browne, The Only Child*

Again, a recurring pattern of thought in the mind is known as a *samskara*. Imagine a kerosene lantern. Without smoke the glass would be clear and the light inside would be able to shine through and illuminate without inteference. Just so, without thoughts (smoke) the true you, open to infinite possibility (the lantern light), would be able to create without limitation. When thoughts come up, they cloud the glass a bit, so the light is less resplendent, as is the ability to create without limitation. When those thoughts become habit or thought patterns and tendencies, those *samskaras* cloud the glass even more. Further, when *samskaras* become deeply ingrained in our personality, they become the obstacles, or *klesas*. And the *klesas* are so solidly ensconced in our character that they can pretty much paralyze us so that we can't even think about creating. The *klesas* are:

Avidya (ignorance)—Ignorance takes on many layers and forms of its own, but the first and most clear form is the belief that we are this body and this mind. Failing to recognize the true, deep, infinite, and undying part of us is the first and purest form of *avidya*.

Asmita (egoism)—This is how we label ourselves. It can be as simple as *I am a woman, I am a man, I am Italian*, or more complex like *I am a very good cook, I am stuck in a job that I hate, I could never make the change in my life that I want, Good things don't happen to people like me*. This is where a lot of the disallowing beliefs either keep us limited or, if worked with, can be changed to open us up to what we want.

Raga (attachment) and *dvesha* (aversion)—Human beings are hardwired for survival, and there is a negativity bias because of this. Our normal reactive patterns are the product of all our conditioning. As part of this conditioning, we are inherently drawn toward certain things and repelled by others. This keeps us in a state of limited perception, which will often keep us from what we are looking to create.

Abhinivesa (fear)—the true definition of *abhinivesa* is clinging to life. We can also look at this as fear of falling or failing. The simple question is: What would you do if you knew you wouldn't fail? Whenever there is fear, it is a sure sign that you are allowing discordant thoughts to run rampant.

The *samskaras* are the individual threads. Woven together, they become the fabric of the *klesas*—the fabric that makes up the blinders keeping our field of perception limited. The *samskaras* and *klesas* keep us from choice in our lives. They keep us from true creativity and from true freedom. The more you both clear the mind and work within a state of mindfulness in your daily life, the more available infinite choice becomes.

This is great to know, because if you have a belief that is not helping to create what you want out of life—a *disallowing* belief—is that the time to throw up your hands and give up? Absolutely not! It is, though, time for you to start working with the disallowing belief . . . time for you to begin playing around with finding a new thought to think over and over again. Neurons in the brain connect to create patterns of thought, establishing patterns of belief. By letting go of thought patterns that no longer serve you and creating new thoughts, you will both prune the old and create new neural networks, networks bolstering beliefs that will both support what you want to create and allow those things into your life. And you can do that. It's what the Vibe-a-Thon is all about. You're on your way to doing it *right now*.

Understand that you need to be a match to what you want. Through what you perceive. Not with your *words*, but with your *vibe*.

Number 3: Show up, do the work and don't give up.

Changing your perception does not happen overnight. Further, the more deeply ingrained the disallowing beliefs, *samskaras*, and *klesas* are regarding what you are looking to create, the more effort it will take to turn the perception around. It WILL happen, but it takes effort.

Sutra 1.14 states that there are three qualities to practice. It must be consistent, must take place over a long period of time, and must be pursued with passion and interest. How long it takes to bring about what you want in your life is dependent on your conditioning and your ability to work to change that. So have patience and interest in the process. You will see how fascinating it is!

Let's say you are in New York and decide to drive to California. You get into the car and begin your journey, knowing that California is somewhere in the distance. When you get halfway across the country and have yet to see any sign indicating that California is coming, would you turn around and go back home? No. You know that California is out there . . . you have only to keep on your path. And as you get closer and closer to your destination, you begin to see signs stating that California is *x* number of miles away.

The closer you get to California, the more signs you see indicating that you are getting there. And the more you line up with what you desire, the more evidence and opportunity will show up for you.

And know this: often, what holds us back from what we want to create are uncontrolled and unidentified disallowing thoughts and beliefs that we aren't even aware of. It's as though we have been driving in circles without any kind of road map, trying in vain to get where we want to go. The great news here is that you are on your way to creating your own map, to steering your life in the direction you want it to go. The more you take responsibility and take on the work, the more clearly the map will read.

I know you can have what you want. I believe in your ability to create with every fiber of my being. And I believe also that you know about vibing, about syncing up with what you want and the process of creation. It's why you opened this book. You are a powerful creator! Whatever you desire in your life, you can have. Just do the work and stay with it. It's not necessarily easy, but I wouldn't say it's hard either. And I promise: it will change your life in wonderful ways.

Exercises for Week One

Exercise #1: Set up your Vibe-a-Thon

What do you want? What sparks the life in you, or what perhaps would you love to experience but feel intimidated to think about? And what is the vibe you are sending out about it? In other words, how do you really feel about it? What are your beliefs about it?

This is a great way to see how you feel about the things you want to manifest in your life. When we start playing around with our thoughts and beliefs in one area of life, it provides the template for other areas. Because a belief is simply a thought you think over and over again. So if you want to change a belief that's holding you back, you need to change the thought. You'll be tweaking your beliefs and changing the way you think to come into alignment in every area of your life in no time.

OK? Great—let's get to it. Take out three sheets of paper . . .

Step one: On the first sheet, write down the subject of your monthlong Vibe-a-Thon. Underneath this, make a list of all the things holding you back from this manifestation.

Example: The thing I would like to work on manifesting in my life through presenting the Vibe-a-Thon as a book is to create a great experience for all the people who are participating. I want it to be interesting and thought provoking, but more than anything else I want it to be exciting and FUN, and to provide a platform for people to take ownership of creating their lives.

What's holding me back?

1. I'm not an expert. I don't have a master's degree or PhD in vibing and am merely going on my own experience and the things that have

helped me in my life. Who am I to talk about this to other people on a scale larger than one-on-one?

2.   This is going to be *work*! I'm going to have to sit down and write this as a book. I will need to be present in my experience on a daily basis. Do I really want to take on this kind of commitment?

3.   I've come up with an idea of something I've wanted to create a million times. And the same thing happens—I get all excited about it and work myself up and then get overwhelmed and completely back off. Who's to say that this will be any different?

Step two: Take the list of things holding you back. On the second sheet of paper, write down each item on the list and next to it create a statement that softens the negativity into a hopeful positive statement. (In other words, begin to change your belief by actually changing the thought).

Statement

I'm not an expert. I don't have a master's degree or PhD in vibing and am merely going on my own experience and the things that I have learned that have helped me in my life. Who am I to talk about this to other people on a scale larger than one-on-one?

BETTER Statement

It doesn't matter where the knowledge comes from. It's important and amazing stuff to know and I am being driven to pass the information on to others. I have had a vast array of experience during my years on earth and I know that my talent lies in communicating to others in a way that they can receive. I care about people, and it will be thrilling to see them begin to create for themselves. I know that in the same way as I have brought in those teachers I was ready to learn from, the people who are meant to have this passed on by me are being brought to the Vibe-a-Thon. And as far as I know, there is no such thing as an advanced degree program in vibing.

This is going to be *work*! I'm going to have to sit down and write this as a book. I will need to be present in my experience on a daily basis. Do I really want to take on this kind of commitment?

For me, there is no better feeling than that of helping somebody "get to" what he or she desires and witnessing their process of easeful creation. I also get a tremendous sense of satisfaction and accomplishment when I go through the process of writing/editing/writing/editing, etc., and finally distilling it down to a finished product that satisfies me, deep down at the very level of my soul. And I will have to be present in the good-feeling, vibrational alignment of creating something wonderful. How can that really be work?

I've come up with an idea of something I've wanted to create a million times. And the same thing happens—I get all excited about it and work myself up and then get overwhelmed and completely back off. Who's to say that this will be any different?

I always said that I would write something when and if I ever figured out what I really wanted to write about. I know this way of living/thinking works, and the passion that I feel will fuel me through the Vibe-a-Thon. Besides, I have not yet had the experience of starting a project like this with all the knowledge of vibing, meditation, mindfulness, and the philosophy of yoga that I now possess. So I'll just hold my vision of how I want this Vibe-a-Thon to go and let it all flow from there. Because I've shown myself in other areas of my life that I can manifest whatever it is that I want, and this is just the latest game I'm bringing to the playground of my life.

Step three: On top of the third sheet of paper, write in big, bold letters I CAN MANIFEST THIS. Underneath that, write the list of the wonderful, hopeful, powerfully vibe-charged things you came up with on the second sheet. Once you have created this page, read it over. Feel the excitement welling up inside of you? This is what it's all about . . . syncing up with your vibration.

Underneath that, write "MY LIFE WITH X IN IT". Write a description of how good you will feel, etc., when you have manifested this thing. And get goofy with it! Remember, this is for your eyes only. Write something that is nice and juicy, so that you can refer back to it and keep your vibe up—for the duration of the Vibe-a-Thon and beyond.

Fold the third sheet of paper and put it in a place where you can access it at a moment's notice (i.e., your wallet). During the course of the week, glance at it from time to time and allow it to feed the vision.

Example:

I CAN MANIFEST THIS.

1. It doesn't matter where the knowledge comes from. It's important and amazing stuff to know and I am being driven to pass the information on to others. I have had a vast array of experience during my years on earth and I know that my talent lies in communicating to others in a way that they can receive. I care about people, and it will be thrilling to see them begin to create for themselves. I know that in the same way as I have brought in those teachers I was ready to learn from, the people who are meant to have this passed on by me are being brought to the Vibe-a-Thon. And as far as I know, there is no such thing as an advanced degree program in vibing.

2. For me, there is no better feeling than that of helping somebody "get to" what he or she desires and witnessing their process of easeful cre-ation. I also get a tremendous sense of satisfaction and accomplishment when I go through the process of writing/editing/writing/editing, etc., and finally distilling it down to a finished product that satisfies

me, deep down at the very level of my soul. And I will have to be present in the good-feeling, vibrational alignment of creating something wonderful. How can that really be work?

3. I always said that I would write something when and if I ever figured out what I really wanted to write about. I know this way of living/thinking works, and the passion that I feel will fuel me through the Vibe-a-Thon. Besides, I have not yet had the experience of starting a project like this with all the knowledge of vibing, meditation, mindfulness, and the philosophy of yoga that I now possess. So I'll just hold my vision of how I want this Vibe-a-Thon to go and let it all flow from there. Because I've shown myself in other areas of my life that I can manifest whatever it is that I want, and this is just the latest game I'm bringing to the playground of my life.

MY LIFE HAVING COMPLETED THE VIBE-A-THON AS A BOOK

Wow! I can't belief it's done. So effortlessly? It makes sense, is fun, and is easy to understand. And in talking to people who have read it, they are not only realizing that they can create whatever it is that they want out of life, but they are really *doing* it. They are getting that yoga is a way of life and understanding just how powerful the tools it provides are. And look at this: The work that I needed to do for this wasn't even what I would call work. It simply flowed out of me and was infinitely fascinating. What a great experience! And I've shown myself what I really have always known—that I can create whatever it is that I want in my life. I just did it! So what do I want to do next? Because this really was cool and great and fun and I want to keep playing with it!

Exercise #2: Meditation

As you now understand, we need to clear the mind as best as we can in order to create the thoughts that are going to lead us toward what we are looking for. Meditation is an integral part of the work of the Vibe-a-Thon, so try your best to be as consistent as possible with it for the course of the month.

Following is a practice of meditation for you to follow. If you have a different practice that you prefer, please use that. What matters is the consistency.

The sessions will incorporate simple breath work to start to focus the mind, followed by internal breath exploration leading to a period of quieting the mind. The session will end with a few minutes of actively visualizing the subject of your Vibe-a-Thon.

Considerations:

1. Wear comfortable clothing and find a comfortable seat. You need to be sitting upright so as not to fall asleep, but if you want a bit more support you can sit against a wall or on a chair.

2. Have a timer that you can set intervals on—this will keep you from guessing how long you've been at it, which will go a long way toward keeping the mind internally focused. There are some great meditation timers out there, and great apps as well.

3. Set a consistent time for meditation. It may be easier for you first thing in the morning, but if you have responsibilities then, maybe afternoon will work better for you. Remember that consistency is the most important thing here, so for the month try to dedicate the same time frame every day.

4. The sessions for week one will last a total of fifteen minutes each. We will expand the time as the weeks go, so that you can work up to longer periods without getting overwhelmed or frustrated. As mentioned above, if you have a practice of sitting already established, stay with your practice.

The Session:

1. 3 minutes—Alternate Nostril Breathing (i.e., *Nadi Shodhana*)

   a. Place your left palm face up on your left thigh with the thumb and forefinger touching (Jnana mudra).

   b. Curl the first two fingers of your right hand into the palm of the hand and bring the right ring finger to the left nostril (just between the hard and soft cartilage), the right thumb to the right nostril (between the hard and soft cartilage). This is how you will alternate the breath in the nostrils.

c. Inhale and exhale calmly once through both nostrils.

d. Close off the left nostril and inhale softly through the right.

e. Close off both nostrils for a moment, and then open the left nostril and exhale softly.

f. Inhale through the left nostril.

g. Close off both nostrils for a moment, and then open the right nostril and exhale softly.

h. Continue the pattern.

i. When the interval timer goes off, release your right hand down to the right thigh, palm facing up. Release the mudra of the left hand, so that both palms are open.

2. 2 minutes—Breath Awareness

a. Without manipulating the breath, be with the experience of the inhalation and exhalation as they move through the body. If you find yourself in a thought, that's OK. Just bring your awareness back to the breath, however many times it happens.

b. To help with focus here, you can silently chant the mantra "so" as you inhale and "hum" as you exhale.

3. 5 minutes—Effortful Concentration (*Dharana*)

a. Bring your attention to a point of focus inside of yourself— anything you choose is fine. Ajna chakra (the third eye point) or Anahata chakra (the heart) are often used.

    b.   Keep your internal gaze softly focused there. When thoughts come up, don't judge or analyze. Just bring yourself back to the point of focus.

    c.   Many people find that repeating a phrase or mantra can help greatly in focusing the mind. If there is a poem, prayer, mantra, or phrase that helps to calm and open your mind, feel free to use that. If you don't have any ideas, here are some suggestions:

        i.   *I am open to infinite possibilities.*

        ii.   *Everything is possible.*

4.   5 minutes—Visualization

    a.   Once the mind has calmed and become a bit more open, bring in the subject of your Vibe-a-Thon. Let the vision get as juicy as you can, to the point where you feel that you are in the real experience of it.

HAVE FUN and BE EASY with it! You can't get it wrong and we are all constantly evolving so you can never get it done . . . but we can (and should) enjoy the creating.

Supplemental information, support and community for vibers can be found online at www.vibeathon.com.

Remember, what you perceive you receive . . . Now, vibe on!

Day Two: It's How You Look at It

And those who were seen dancing were thought to be insane by those who could not hear the music.

~ attributed to Friedrich Wilhelm Nietzsche

I had a telling moment, some time ago. Ending a full day of teaching by taking a great class, I was exhausted but rejuvenated and completely relaxed. It was raining out—pouring actually—and humid. I began my walk home along the outside edge of Central Park, but it looked so uninhabited and lovely within that I entered.

Since the park's weekend rules prohibited cars on the road, I shared the street with only one or two diligent runners. The street was black and shiny from the rain and there were some leaves on the ground. And though there were no cars, the traffic lights were still going. Green . . . yellow . . . red. Each light kept its time, reflecting onto the street for what seemed my sole enjoyment. It was so peaceful and beautiful, and I felt that I was being given a wonderful gift. I walked a half hour out of my way, so absorbed in the moment. What a great, great experience.

Two days later, it was still raining. My day was just as busy as the one previously described, but the effect of the rain was completely different. I made my way through the park, retracing the exact path I had taken and getting increasingly agitated with each step. It was dark and rainy and nothing more than a big pain in the butt!

What a lesson! Same intensity of rain . . . the street was still black and shiny . . . some leaves were on the street . . . and my beloved park was again closed to traffic. The same exact circumstance! What changed?

What changed was my *perception* of the situation, that's all. We are ever-changing beings—really, as changeable as the weather. The energy inside of us is in a constant dance, and the incessant flux can cause us to be in a different frame of mind. Think about it. What are some of the influences that might change your viewpoint? Having a bad night of sleep, ingesting too much coffee, having just completed a tiring day at work, or having had a wonderful one, making your way home to share a meal with people you love. Our state of mind sets the tone for how we perceive. And the further away from an open state of mind that our moods drive us, the more strongly the ego confines us within a limited perception. And so, we seek out evidence that is in line with where our perception currently is.

In her book, *Positivity*, Dr. Barbara Fredrickson outlines two core truths regarding positive and negative perspectives and how they shape our emotional well-being and ability to create.

1. Positivity opens us. The first core truth about positive emotions is that they open our hearts and our minds, making us more receptive and more creative.[12]

2. Positivity transforms us for the better. This is the second core truth about positive emotions. By opening our hearts and minds, positive emotions allow us to discover and build new skills, new ties, new knowledge, and new ways of being.[13]

Negative emotions narrow our thinking, our ability to see possibilities, and our ability to problem solve. It's like spiraling down the rabbit hole, like being confined by limitations and boundaries and having no visible way out.

Unless and until we take the mindful approach of looking at our thoughts and emotional states and actively changing them so they reflect a more peaceful state, we will continue to be a slave to the mind. By cultivating a state of presence—of being here and clear in the present moment—we can experience the thoughts and moods as the transient states they are and move beyond them.

Things are never bad; it's the way you think about them.

~ Epictetus

---

12   Barbara Fredrickson, *Positivity*, p. 21
13   Ibid., p. 24

In the park, when I realized that my perception was skewed and took a moment to look down at the shiny black street again, it didn't look beautiful right away. But by doing the work of looking at and clearing the thoughts associated with what I didn't want (in this case, a grumpy walk home), by the time I left the park my appreciation level was just as high as it had been on that earlier walk.

One afternoon, I took an asana class. This class in particular presented another great example of how differently our perspectives can shape our experiences.

During the class, the teacher had us explore Adho Mukha Svanasana (downward facing dog) with our head on a block. We first examined the pose with the crown of the head on the block, then the forehead. Afterward, she asked four of the students to describe the specific effect on their bodies. For each of the four, the answer was different: one student felt the effect in her thoracic spine; I felt it in my sacrum; another experienced it in her shoulders; and the last felt it in her neck. Was one correct and the others wrong? No! These were all the different issues we had been dealing with individually, so our perspective was geared toward our own experience.

All reality is perceived. The way that we look at something is colored by our previous conditioning and experiences and the validation or rejection associated with them. When we understand that the attention we give to something is simply a thought, then it makes sense that by changing our thoughts we can change our perception. Changing our perception changes how we interact, thus shaping our experiences. Then we are changing our reality. Creating our daily lives must be an active choice. It will not happen by default.

> *Destiny is not the path given to us; it's the path we choose to take.*
>
> *~ Megamind*

Isn't it amazing what a little attitude adjustment can do? And if a short walk in the park can turn the day around, imagine how a shift in perspective can help with the things you're looking to create!

For Today:

1. Continue with meditation.

2. For consideration: Take some time today and look honestly at your perspective regarding the subject of your Vibe-a-Thon. To help you, contemplate the following:

   a. Does your ability to vibe on what you are looking to create waver from good and possible to humiliatingly impossible?

   b. In both the moments of good and humiliating impossibility, try to stay present with everything that is going on in both your internal and external worlds. Are you reacting to what's happening around you? Are you getting *caught up* in what's happening around you?

This is all entirely normal and human, but our work is to learn how not to react to the things that are keeping us from lining up with what we want. The first step toward doing that is to witness what's going on. Your vibe may still waver, and that's OK. Just see if you can identify the elements that are causing the change inside of you first. Once identified, you can start to soften the reaction. With time, the reaction will disappear.

Supplemental information, support and community for vibers can be found online at www.vibeathon.com.

Remember, what you perceive you receive . . . Now, vibe on!

Day Three: Are You the Sun or the Wind?

Even after all this time

The Sun never says to the earth,

"You owe me"

Look what happens with a

love like that,

It lights the Whole Sky.

~ Hafiz[14]

There's an old tale of the Sun and the Wind. One day, as they hung out up in the sky looking down at the comings and goings of the world and sipping lattes, they spotted a man wearing an overcoat. As it was a slow weather day, boredom led each to challenge the other to a contest. The winner would be the one who got the coat removed; the loser would pay for the lattes.

The Wind went first. It blew and blew but the man merely clutched his coat more tightly.

Then the Sun took a turn. As its warmth beamed down, the coat soon came off.

How's the vibing going? Are you staying in a fun, good-feeling place of happy expectation with regard to what you are in the process of creating? Are you beginning to see how this is just as much an internal journey that we're on, and not solely an action journey?

In *How Quantum Activism Can Save Civilization*, Dr. Amit Goswami discusses the concepts of upward and downward causation. Upward causation is based on

14   Daniel Ladinsky, *The Gift: Poems by Hafiz, The Great Sufi Master*, p. 34

the notion that "elementary particles make atoms, atoms make molecules, molecules make cells, cells make brain, and brain makes consciousness."[15] In this view, manifestation comes through interaction, or by *doing*. With downward causation, creativity and manifestation of what we desire begins with consciousness, specifically *with consciousness choosing from its own possibilities*. Goswami says, "the state of consciousness from which we choose is more subtle than the mind-set when you are actively out there, in your normal mind state and world. It's a non-ordinary state of interconnected consciousness in which all beings are one, a 'higher' quantum consciousness. Hence the appropriateness of calling causation from it 'downward' and the source 'God.' "

Since downward causation starts from consciousness and comes to actuality from the field of infinite possibilities available, the more open the mind is the more freely we can perceive evidence that we are moving in the right direction, discern contrast to help us further clarify what we do want, and notice opportunities to take active steps toward what we are looking to create. This is the necessary piece of the creativity pie that most people are missing. Once we get our vibe up to speed, *then* we employ upward causation and take action.

Creativity is not all in the mind, nor is it all in the work. It's a combination of both *being* and *doing*. The creative process is a joint effort of the do mode (which is left brain and interested in details) and be mode (with the right brain's ability to open to possibilities and create outside the box). As Goswami (and Sinatra and Scooby Doo) say:

"DO BE DO BE DO!"

This is clearly understood within the philosophy of yoga in sutras 1.15 and 1.16, which describe the concepts of *abhyasa* (practice) and *vairagya* (nonattachment). Practice is sustained effort toward anything—from a particular point of focus to the subject of your Vibe-a-Thon, and further to all levels of relating in your world. *Abhyasa* is active and balanced out by *vairagya*, which represents the ability to let go, to be unattached to the outcome or result.

As modern-day human beings, we are more comfortable with and geared toward *abhyasa*, or *do* mode than *be* mode, *vairagya*. Through the work of the

---

15   Amit Goswami, *How Quantum Activism Can Save Civilization*, p. 56

Vibe-a-Thon, you are bringing balance back from "DO DO DO DO DO" to "DO BE DO BE DO." And DO BE DO BE DO sounds much better with music, don't you think? So, for now imagine yourself as the Sun. Vibrating, radiant energy beaming onto your desire, warming it into being by doing the internal work to line up vibrationally.

For Today:

1. Continue with meditation.

2. For consideration: Are you more like the Sun or the Wind in your daily life?

    a. Like the Sun: Is your first impulse to sit and visualize what you want to create in your life? Do you find that you are really great at visualizing but have a hard time taking action toward what you want?

    b. Like the Wind: If there is something you are looking to create, is your first impulse to try to get it done? Or do you take the time to see it through in your mind first?

Whichever one resonates for you more clearly, spend some time in the mode that will balance it out. If you tend to be more of a doer, take a few extra moments in visualizing yourself in the good-feeling place of already having what you are working to create. If you tend to visualize more than act, look to identify even the slightest opportunity to be more active in your creation. Have fun!

Supplemental information, support and community for vibers can be found online at www.vibeathon.com.

Remember, what you perceive you receive . . . Now, vibe on!

Day Four: Can I get a Witness?

How's it going? Are you in the blissful state of aligning your vibration with your desire? Are you playing with the understanding that you can create what you want by following these simple steps?

1. Decide what you want.

2. Line up with your aspiration vibrationally.

3. Show up, do the internal work—take in the evidence that validates that you are on the right path, contrast showing you what you don't want to bring you to further clarity about what you do want, and op-portunities to make it happen—and don't give up!

Once you've decided on what you want and are in the process of lining up through meditation and mindfulness in your daily life, do you need to spend every waking moment holding the vision in some form of mental death grip? Not at all! That mental death grip is, in actuality, the ego keeping us in the habitual patterns of thought and locked in our old perceptions, where the new stuff can't get in. When working to open the mind to the infinite field of possibilities, it's important to remember that you are opening yourself up to perceptions that are beyond what you have experienced before. This can be in the form of new opportunities, ideas, and ways of thinking.

So, exactly what are thoughts, and how do they contribute to the realities that we experience? Let's look again at the example of a movie screen. If we think of our deepest Self (our Soul, higher Self, Universal Consciousness, etc.) as the movie screen, sans projection, it is pure, calm, peaceful, unaffected, and undisturbed.

Our thoughts are the projections onto that screen. Every flavor and color of thought presents itself on the mind, from what you consider to be good thoughts to the more challenging thoughts that often cause anxiety and move-ment away from what you are trying to create.

Some of those thoughts could be considered more harmful than others, agreed? Further, some of our thoughts are conscious (like the dance number in a musical that draws our attention), others more subliminal (the innocuous person sitting at the bar in one scene who turns out to be the villain scenes later).

Does it make sense that without the ability to control and direct our thoughts toward the type of projections (and perceptions) that we choose, the screen can seem like a bad movie montage gone crazy?

On the flip side, if we can distinguish and cultivate our thoughts so that they are in line with the lives we wish to create, the possibilities are endless.

Through the practice of meditation, we try to focus our attention away from the myriad of thoughts, to sit in a space of peace for a period of time. We learn first to become witness to the chatter in the mind. Then, as we continue to draw attention toward our point of focus, the chatter appears to die down. The mind is open, calmer, still. And in witnessing the expansive calm, the blinders limiting our perception peel away and we can enter into the field of infinite possibility. Our perspective opens up, and the beginnings of true creativity can take place.

Meditation is the training field, and life is where the dance takes place. The human species has evolved through survival of the fittest, and our assumed natural inclination has developed to react first and fix things later. Living the path of creativity through yoga takes us away from the reactive habits of stimulus and immediate response. Through the practice of yoga as a lifestyle, we come to understand the true nature of our lives: we are spiritual beings involved in a human experience.

> *If we consider what happens in conversation, in reveries, in remorse, in times of passion, in surprises, in instructions of dreams, wherein often we see ourselves in masquerade—the droll disguises only magnifying and enhancing a real element and forcing it on our distant notice—we shall catch many hints that will broaden and lighten into knowledge of the secret of nature. All goes to show that the soul in man is not an organ, but animates and exercises all the organs; is not a function, like the power of memory, of calculation, of comparison, but uses these as hands and feet; is not a faculty but a light; is not*

the intellect or the will; is the background of our being, in which they lie—an immensity not possessed and that cannot be possessed. From within or from behind, a light shines through us upon things and makes us aware that we are nothing, but the light is all. A man is the façade of a temple wherein all wisdom and all good abide. What we commonly call man, the eating, drinking, planting, counting man, does not, as we know him, represent himself, but misrepresents himself. Him we do not respect, but the soul, whose organ he is, would he let it appear through his action, would make our knees bend. When it breathes through his intellect, he is genius; when it breathes through his will, it is virtue; when it flows through his affection, it is love. And the blindness of the intellect begins when it would be something of itself. The weakness of the will begins when the individual would be something of himself. All reform aims in some one particular to let the soul have its way through us; in other words, to engage us to behave.

~ Ralph Waldo Emerson, "The Over-Soul"

Our ability to stay in a place of witnessing—to take a step back before we react, to understand that such a reaction is nothing more than our habitual response, to then decide whether or not the habitual response is in line with what we are looking to create, and to act from there—is the first step toward creating anything. The more we recognize ourselves as spiritual beings within the dance of human experience, the more our lives can shine forth from that place of limitlessness that connects us all.

For Today:

1. Continue with meditation.

2. For consideration: Through the course of your day today, play around with being witness to your thoughts. While at work, in conversation with people you are close to or with the salesperson ringing up a purchase for you. Is there some level of reaction? If so, can you take a step back from the reaction, experience it, decide if it's in line with the way you're learning to cultivate thoughts and then potentially change the reaction?

Supplemental information, support and community for vibers can be found online at www.vibeathon.com.

Remember, what you perceive you receive . . . Now, vibe on!

Day Five: Keep Your Eyes on the Prize (and Don't Get Caught Up in the Details)

Many years ago, a young woman was making her way in the Big City. (Let's call her, oh, I don't know, Jeanmarie). Jeanmarie had been living with a roommate for a number of years and was ready to move into her own apartment. Her limited budget was seemingly at odds with the vision she held—a decent sized one bedroom that she could call home. Having learned a bit about creating life by how we think, Jeanmarie was undaunted as she began looking at the closets that were available in her price range. She persevered, holding the vision of what she wanted and keeping her eye on the prize. And though the apartments she saw seemed to get smaller and smaller, she kept working to expand her mind, opening herself to possibility.

She vibed on.

A week or so into her search, Jeanmarie was having lunch with a friend in the cafeteria where she worked. A coworker was seated next to her, discussing with a mutual friend the fact that she needed to move back to Germany and was desperate to find someone to take over the lease on her apartment. Without hesitation, Jeanmarie introduced herself to the woman and asked about the apartment. Not only was the apartment a one bedroom, the rent was exactly the amount that Jeanmarie had been paying in her previous place! Within two days, she had signed the lease . . . and is still happily in her home, now many years later.

Our awareness is atomic, *eka grata* or one-pointed in nature. Most believe the mind is capable of taking on a number of things at the same time, to the point where "multitasking" is a skill most believe we both have in spades and are highly capable of honing. But more and more research is making it evident that the opposite is true: our minds are in fact only able to focus on one thing at a time, and multitasking means that we take on many things and give them all the same, poor degree of attention.

Our awareness has the nature of a point. This allows us to direct it in specific ways, and at the same time gives it a tendency to become narrow, attaching us to repetitive patterns of thought, or *samskaras*. When we stay within the same cycles of thought, it's as though the blinders limiting our field of perception—and thus, constraining possibility—become ever stronger.

We can focus our attention in two ways. Through the left brain we concentrate on the details, the nitty-gritty of what we're trying to create. Through the right brain, we take in the big picture, and perceive it as a whole. Just as a dot of lavender oil can perfume the entire body with its fragrance, the right brain can see the entirety of a situation and motivate us toward what we desire.

One of the most challenging parts of creating something new is allowing the right brain to convince us—to the depths of our being—that it is possible. The chatter of the left brain questions the validity of what we are looking to create and we get caught up in wondering if we even deserve to have what we want.

These disallowing beliefs are part of our conditioning, that's all. And yet we are often convinced that this habituated conditioning toward what we don't want is firmly rooted in reality. Which it is for the most part, unless and until we change the disallowing belief.

On top of that, the evidence that we find as we start the process of vibing often seems like proof *against* what we want to create; it seems to underscore the *impossibility* of opportunity.

And that, my friends, is the moment to take a step back, take a deep breath, get to a place where you can see the big picture of what you are looking to create and know that the less-than-perfect evidence in front of you is the result of your perspective beginning to open up, but your mind still wanting to keep you limited because *that's what it knows for sure, so that's what it can control.*

When seeing the less-than-perfect evidence in our current limited perspective, we actually soften because it's within the ego's realm of comfort. Expanding our perspective is scary, because we have to let go of the boundaries that have held us up, even if those boundaries have held us back. The energy underlying expansion can feel strangely similar to anxiety if we are not attuned to what it truly represents. As we release the anchor and sail over the edge of the waterfall into expansion, our perspective will have us shrieking either with joy or with fear.

Learning to balance in an inversion illustrates the challenging process of expanding our perspective. When a student first learns how to come up into Sirsasana (headstand), she often begins at the wall. After learning the setup of the arms and hands and the proper muscular work in the shoulders and back so as to protect the neck, the student lifts up. Tentatively at first, then more clearly over time, she learns to take the legs away from the wall and balance. Interestingly, when the student no longer needs the wall at all for headstand and comes to the center of the room to give it a try, more often than not the first few attempts she either can't come up, falls over immediately, or comes up with a very shaky balance. What happened? She didn't need the wall any longer, yet as soon as she came away from it all the work seems to come undone!

The idea of the wall was, in effect, keeping the blinders limiting the student's perspective locked in place. Knowing that it was there allowed the student's mind to open up to balancing because the wall was there to catch her if she fell. She opened her field of possibility to include balancing *with the wall* whether she needed its support or not. When the student came away from the wall, her ego had to expand further into the confidence that there was no longer any need for support.

Coming back to the experience of finding my apartment, when I began the depressing process of looking at places and finding nothing that was close to what I was vibing on, I had a conscious choice to make. I could delve into the pessimism and keep my perspective focused on not getting what I wanted, or I could disregard what was unfortunately in front of me, keep my eyes on the prize and carry on. Further, instead of looking at what I didn't want as evidence that my desires were unrealizable, I learned to look at it as *contrast* that could more specifically elucidate just what I did want. Each apartment that I didn't want provided the opportunity to get clarity on exactly what I did want. In that way, the detail-oriented part of my brain was able to start opening up to the bigger picture. The borders of perspective opened, et voilà!

This was one of the first times in my life where I actively did the internal work to create what I wanted. And though there were some mild moments of doubt,

I stayed in the process. And not only did it work out, but it became one of the experiences that I go back to as evidence that I can create. And so can you.

For Today:

1. Continue with meditation.

2. For consideration: We have all had experiences when things seemed to find a way of working out. See if you can think of a few times this has happened to you—in big or small ways. The more evidence you can gather about how you have brought things into manifestation, the more inspired you will become to create your life more consciously (now that you are learning how to do that).

Supplemental information, support and community for vibers can be found online at www.vibeathon.com.

Remember, what you perceive you receive. . . Now, vibe on!

Day Six: The Big BUT!

No, that's not a misspelling . . .

Often, as we set something we want to create into motion by vibing on it, we remove the possibility of it ever happening in the very same moment. How? With use of the big, ever pervasive BUT!

Imagine you want to take a vacation to Bora-Bora (and who wouldn't want to take a vacation to Bora-Bora?). You make the statement *I want to go to Bora-Bora on vacation, but there's no way I can make that happen.* You have given birth to your desire for the vacation, and in the same breath removed the possibility of creating it with the statement *there's no way I can make that happen.* In actuality, you become a vibrational match to no way of making it happen.

Much of what we wish to create is voided in that exact way.

How we think has direct ramifications on the course and shape our lives take. Thoughts are vibrational and light in nature. If you have a thought only once and then it is gone, that particular thought will most likely not have a significant impact on you. However, habitual thoughts become patterns of thinking or *samskaras* that take on an emotional charge and ultimately turn into a belief. Beliefs and emotionally charged thoughts become more and more dense, and can bring actual physical changes to our reality.

Need some proof of this? Your wish is my command! Actually, not mine but the work of a profoundly inspiring scientist, Masaru Emoto. Dr. Emoto has taken thousands of photographs exploring the vibrational effect of words on water. In his experiments, he taped specific words to the bottom of water bottles, studying the formation of the water crystals that develop as a result of the *vibrational charge of the words.* Using high-speed photography, Dr. Emoto discovered that crystals formed in frozen water reveal changes when specific, concentrated thoughts are directed toward them. He found that water from clear springs and water that has been exposed to loving words show brilliant, complex, and colorful snowflake patterns. In contrast, polluted water, or water exposed to negative thoughts, forms incomplete, asymmetrical patterns with dull colors.

Skeptical? Check this out! The first photo (below) is a frozen water sample from the lake at Fujiwara dam in Japan.

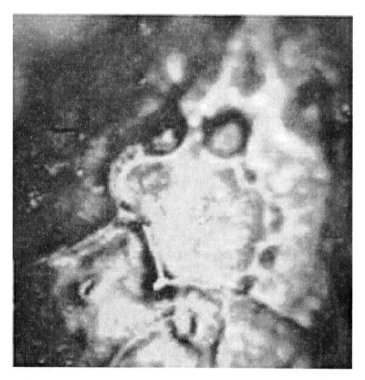

(C) Office Masaru Emoto, LLC

After taking the first sample, a high priest from the local temple prayed for an hour next to the dam. The sample that was taken afterward is shown next. The mud-colored, unshaped sample changed to a bright hexagon. Isn't that magnificent?

(C) Office Masaru Emoto, LLC

If human beings are made up of approximately 80 percent water, can you see how important it is to be conscious of what you say or think about the desire you're vibing on?

We have all had the experience of energy in our lives. A friend walks into the room and we can instantly "feel" that they are in a bad mood, or that something has happened. We wake up in the morning with a weird sense about someone or something, only to find later on that our sense was accurate. We are vibrational in nature. Our physical bodies are merely a densification of energy, and our thoughts and emotions have the same ability to affect the world outside of us as words have to affect Dr. Emoto's water crystals.

Need more proof? In 1993, Jacobo Grinberg-Zylberbaum, a neurophysicist at the University of Mexico performed an experiment in which he attempted to demonstrate a link between two correlated brains. In other words, he tried to prove that two people could meditate together with successful, direct communication. His experiment was intended to collect empirical scientific evidence through objective machines, and not simply reflect the subjective experience of the participants.

In the experiment, the two subjects meditated in the same room, focused on the intention of unifying their energy. After twenty minutes, they were separated while still continuing their unifying intention. They were placed in individual electromagnetically impenetrable chambers and each subject's brain was wired up to an electroencephalogram (EEG) machine.

Subject A was shown a series of light flashes that produced activity in the brain, which showed up on the EEG. After a computer eliminated evidence of brain activity that is not important to mental function, the remaining activity showed up as the same brain activity in subject B. The activity produced in subject A's brain seemed to be transferred to subject B's.

Our perception is the culmination of our thoughts! In order to create, we need to examine what our true thought patterns are with respect to that which we desire. In meditation and mindfulness, unseen patterns become visible, but in fact they were active subliminally all along. Once we reorganize the chatter we can clearly see factors that held us back. What is seemingly complex is, in reality, quite simple:

> *You are what your deep, driving desire is.*

> *As your desire is, so is your will.*

> *As your will is, so is your deed.*

> *As your deed is, so is your destiny.* (Brihadaranyaka Upanishad IV.4.5)[16]

For Today:

1. Continue with meditation.

---

16   Eknath Easwaran, *The Upanishads*, p. 6

2. For consideration: Take that big old "but" out of the equation! Give it a shot with what you're vibing on. What kind of statements are you making, to yourself or to others? Are there some big buts in there that you need to change? What are you waiting for?

Supplemental information, support and community for vibers can be found online at www.vibeathon.com.

Remember, what you perceive you receive . . . Now, vibe on!

Day Seven: What Are You Looking At?

If you want to go east, don't walk toward the west.

~ Sri Ramakrishna

Are you keeping your thoughts and perspective focused toward what you want to create, or what you currently perceive as your reality—toward what "*is*"? When we give most of our attention to what "*is*," the perspective stays trained on what "*is*." And then the blinders that our ego has wrapped around our current perception hold fast, providing us nothing more than evidence of and opportunity to create more of what we currently perceive. The experiences may seem unconnected—different places, different faces—but on closer inspection it's all stemming from the same vibrational proclivity.

Let's use the example of Bob, who is having a hard time financially, trying to vibe on more money but has yet to find relief:

- Bob observes the lack of money he is experiencing. He looks at the bills, the mortgage and car payments, the dwindling amount of cash that he has for the things he and his family need. He wants to be in a better situation, but his mind keeps circulating and percolating on his lack of financial security. He focuses on what "*is*" so his perception stays within those boundaries. And so, he perceives more evidence of his lack and more opportunity to experience more of the lack, as he stays focused on what his current perception is.

- Although there is infinite possibility available to Bob with respect to his finances, the fact that he is only looking at his financial lack keeps his perspective limited to the lack. In effect, there is a whole pile of treasure directly behind him, but since he's focused on what he doesn't have right in front of him he can't see what's available. His mind is closed off to it.

— As a result, Bob's world continues to spiral in the direction of lack. Bills that he forgot about come in, extra work that he was hoping for falls through, etc. Since his perspective is focused on lack of money, his mind is going to look for more evidence of the lack and more opportunity to prove that he is in a place of lack. In arguing for his limitation, that is what he continues to receive.

When we look only at what "*is*," we get more of what "*is*" . . . which we observe, and the perspective stays wrapped up in what "*is*," so the mind actively seeks out more evidence of and opportunity to prove what "*is*" and we get more of what "*is*" . . . which we observe, and the perspective stays wrapped up in what "*is*," so the mind actively seeks out more evidence of and opportunity to prove what "*is*" and we get more of what "*is*" . . . which we observe and . . . I could go on and on here, but I think you get the idea.

During the tenth anniversary of the terrorist attacks on the World Trade Center, a documentary aired profiling a group of firemen who had participated in and survived the rescue effort, both during and in the days that followed. In explaining the effects of post-traumatic stress from the event on their lives, one fireman described experiences that so clearly illustrate what we are talking about. He spoke of his inability to move beyond the trauma, of continually finding the numbers 343 (representing the number of firemen who perished in the buildings) and 911 (representing, of course, the date of the attacks) on everything and anything. If he was driving, he would find those numbers on a license plate. He would look at the clock at specifically those times. His perception was still so deeply entrenched within the ramifications of the specific trauma that he continually re-created it for himself. His mind sought out evidence of the trauma, which reinforced the trauma, which caused him to seek out further evidence of the trauma. And so on.

This is simply how the brain works. Neurons that fire together, wire together, creating the patterns of thought that confine us. Through the practice of meditation and mindfulness, we strive to lessen the effects of deeply held patterns of thought on our internal peace and on the external lives that we create. In meditation, we train the mind to focus away from the scattered activity that is, in reality, nothing more than impressions we falsely identify with. As we work more with mindfulness in our daily, external lives, the potential to change how we perceive any stimulus, impulse, budding reaction, or experience becomes more accessible. In order to make those changes so that they are in line with what we are looking to create and move us away from habitual tendencies, we need to develop some *tapas*.

And, no, I don't mean those delicious little Spanish appetizers!

Tapas is one of the tenets of *kriya yoga*, described by Patanjali as the yoga of action. *Kriya yoga* brings the philosophy of yoga to life through practice in all of our experiences in the day-to-day world. It provides us with tools to view all challenges as opportunity to gain clarity surrounding the vision we are holding, and support for us in fine-tuning our vibe when frustration with the process comes up.

Tapas, the first of the three principles of *kriya yoga*, is defined as heat, a burning desire, and that which burns away all impurities. It is the ability to withstand the intensity of something for the power of purification or transformation, to hold on when the easier way out would be to simply forget about it and walk the other way.

We have all practiced *tapas* in our lives, even though we may not have had a term to label it. In the body, any moment of intense physical work that we stick with—even though it's hard and our minds are screaming to stop—is a moment of *tapas*. In addition, in our most intimate relationships we experience and practice *tapas*. In times of conflict, when you would rather walk away and put the situation out of your conscious mind but stay in the heat of the conflict and deal because you know that it will make the relationship stronger, you are practicing *tapas*.

The practice of *tapas* is how we can develop the ability to be steadfast to the vision of what we want, especially when the dark side starts to rear its ugly head in the form of negative thoughts, doubts, and disallowing beliefs.

> *The ultimate measure of a person is not where they stand in moments of comfort and convenience, but where they stand in times of challenge and controversy.*
>
> *~ Dr. Martin Luther King Jr.*

Reflecting back on the example of Bob, is he financially trapped forever? Of course not. With a bit of understanding about clearing the mind through meditation and staying with the thoughts that will change his perspective—even in those very challenging times when the evidence seems to be pointing away from the financial security he desires—Bob can begin on the path of moving toward what he is looking to create. Let's look, shall we?

— Bob is lining up, working on his vision of paying his bills on time and easily with enough of a cushion for his entire family to live freely. As the bills come in, instead of allowing the anxiety (and negativity) to pour in, Bob takes a deep breath, comes back to the focus on what he wants and stays with that until he feels lined up again. (He observes what he *desires* . . . and in observing what he *desires*, he opens his perspective to include the possibility of what he *desires*.)

— Through meditation and mindfulness in his daily life, Bob's perspective begins to open up more and more. He sees that in reality he is not where he would like to be yet, but has enough today for his entire family to live in a level of modest comfort. In focusing on the present moment from a place of clarity and not one of anxiety, he realizes that things are OK. In fact, Bob is creating new neural pathways in support of what he is looking to create, and dissolving the old habits of thought that no longer serve him. And since we are wired to seek out evidence of our beliefs, in changing his perspective he is actively reshaping his life.

— Bob's world begins to ease up. As he focuses on what he wants and stays in that place of vibing while paying what he can for now, little things start to happen: the extra work that had fallen through in the previous example is now available; he receives notification from the electric company stating that they had been charging him too much and will issue a reimbursement; he finds $20 on the street. And this seemingly small good fortune will persist and increase as Bob continues to show up in terms of his vision, do the work, and stay the course.

This is not magic. Magic is for illusionists. Illusion is slave to manipulated, limited perception. Reality is perceived, but we can change our perception by honing our vibe and opening beyond our limited perception. Vibing is for creators!

For Today:

1. Continue with meditation.

2. For consideration: *Tapas* provides a fantastic way of both perceiving and responding to challenges and experiences of life, by embracing them as a guide or teacher. Take some time today to contemplate how you handle the practice of *tapas*.

    a. How do you respond when (trying to) endure a physical challenge? For example, if you practice asana, what happens when you hold a pose for a longer period of time than is "comfortable" for you? Do you come out of the pose? Do you try to "fix" something? Do you get angry or frustrated at the teacher? Or do you experience a sensation of being what some might call "in the zone"? (The same questions can be asked relative to any physical challenge.)

    b. Bring up a past experience of challenge within a relationship. It can be any type of relationship. During the challenge, were you able to stay "in it," or did you honor the desire to run?

    c. Look at the subject of your Vibe-a-Thon. What are you envisioning in terms of what you are trying to create? And when the tendency in the mind is to take the potentially not-so-good evidence and run with it, are you able to take a deep breath and get your vibe back in a manner that is supporting what you want?

Supplemental information, support and community for vibers can be found online at www.vibeathon.com.

Remember, what you perceive you receive . . . Now, vibe on!

Week Two

One evening, an old Cherokee told his grandson about a battle that goes on inside people. He said, "My son, the battle is between two wolves inside us all.

"One is evil—it is anger, envy, jealousy, sorrow, regret, greed, arrogance, self-pity, guilt, resentment, inferiority, lies, false pride, superiority, and ego.

"The other is good—it is joy, peace, love, hope, serenity, humility, kindness, benevolence, empathy, generosity, truth, compassion, and faith."

The grandson thought about it for a minute and then asked his grandfather, "Which wolf wins?"

The old Cherokee simply replied, "The one you feed."

~ Cherokee legend

Here we are, week two! How's it going? Are you vibing? Are you enjoying the view as you begin to open your field of perception to include evidence of and opportunity for that which you are looking to create in your life? Are you starting to view contrast as evidence of what you *don't* want to further clarify what you *do* want? Is your vibration aligning with the subject of your Vibe-a-Thon to the point where you know it's simply a matter of time before making it reality? Are you in a place emotionally where you're not concerned with when it becomes manifest because in the present moment it *feels so good*?

Or are you having a bit of trouble getting to that place of easy expectation?

Not to worry. Help is on the way!

We're on an internal, *emotional* journey, not solely an external, *active* one. And so, in order to sync up vibrationally with what you desire, you need to adjust how you feel about it, which can greatly affect and be affected by the types of thoughts you are thinking.

It's easy to vibe when the mood is good and things are going well in other aspects of our lives, but what if they're not? What if you're having a bad day or the thoughts in your head are keeping you in such a state of what is currently perceived as *reality*—because the mind has not yet expanded to fully encompass what you are creating—that you can't possibly conceive of anything you desire coming to fruition? What then?

It's time to start paying attention to the two points on the vibrational spectrum that are occurring within you constantly. On one end of the spectrum is the subject of your Vibe-a-Thon, which is available to you because all things are possible when you open your field of perception and take mindful steps towards active creation. Next, there's the point on the vibrational spectrum representing where you are in terms of your current thoughts. Combine those thoughts with your emotional stance, and you get a pretty accurate snapshot of your vibration.

To hone our vibe, we need to understand the relationship between the desire and the current belief associated with the desire, and to begin to take note of where we truly are on that vibrational spectrum. The two points are essential for understanding any sort of guidance. Because you need to know where you are—and where it is that you wish to be—in order to begin the journey.

I rented a car one day to drive to my sister's house. I plugged my desired destination into the GPS, and it examined the two points of relativity (where I was starting from and where I was going) in order to devise the most efficient route.

The system considered where I was *in relationship to* where I wanted to be and came up with the route. And then I had a visual and verbal description of how to get where I wanted to be.

Halfway across the George Washington Bridge I decided to make a detour and say hi to my mom. To get to my sister's house I needed to follow the path programmed into the system—staying straight after the bridge and getting onto Route 4. But to visit my mom, I needed to veer right off the bridge onto the Palisades Parkway. Which I did . . . much to the chagrin of the GPS. It began

firmly commanding me "Please return to the highlighted route." "PLEASE RE-
TURN TO THE HIGHLIGHTED ROUTE!"

It could obviously tell that, from where I was in relationship to where I wanted
to go, I was off my path.

We have a much more sophisticated, beautifully intuitive navigational system
within us. Our emotions let us know, in every moment, if our vibe is in alignment with what we are looking to create in our lives. The more in tune you
get with your emotions through meditation and mindfulness, the more adept
you will become at identifying where you are on the vibrational spectrum. It
is then possible to make active changes to the way you are thinking and feeling
and to move in the direction of what you want.

When you say to yourself *I'm not worthy* or *I'm insufficient* or *I'm wrong for wanting this* or *I can't have that*, the negative emotion that you feel is your inner
guidance saying "Please return to the highlighted route," because you have
moved off your path.

In the Yoga Sutras, Patanjali discusses *vikshepa*, the distractions that keep us
from our practice and away from the focus necessary to open the boundaries of our perception to include the realm of experience and opportunity that
provides what we are looking for. They appear in sutra 1.30 as a downward
spiral, consisting of sickness, mental laziness, doubt, lack of enthusiasm, sloth,
craving for sense pleasure, false perception, failure to reach firm ground, and
backsliding. In his eloquent translation, Rev. Jaganath Carrera states "*Vikshepa*,
translated as 'distraction,' means false projection, scattering, dispersing, and
shaking (of the mind stuff). Vikshepa suggests that the obstacles are symptoms
of lack or loss of focus. Again and again, we see why the ability to attain a clear,
focused mind is the cornerstone of the spiritual, creative life."[17]

The enthusiasm we bring to the first few days of anything often succumbs to
the downward spiral of *vikshepa*. For example, during the course of the Vibe-a-
Thon you may feel inspiration waning because you haven't yet manifested what
you are looking to create. Perhaps you've been diligent in your morning meditation, but then one day decide that the bit of sluggishness you feel permits you

17   Jaganath Carrera, *Inside The Yoga Sutras*, p. 72

to stay in bed. As you move through the day, you decide to take the full day off from all work on vibing and allow yourself to return to the reactive patterns you had started to become aware of, wondering what ever made you think you could create what you want in your life. With each moment, you move further and further from the ground you had gained in opening up your field of perception, and the blinders snap easily back into place.

This happens! It's part of the process of being human and may be attributed to what positive psychology defines as ego depletion. Ego depletion refers to the idea that self-control or willpower draws upon a limited pool of mental resources that can be used up. Ego, in this case, is thought of as psychic energy, psychological resources, and mental reserves.

We have a finite amount of willpower that becomes depleted as we use it. What's more, we use the same stock of willpower for all manner of tasks. So when we become singularly focused on one thing for a period of time—say, the subject of a Vibe-a-Thon—our willpower becomes depleted. The promptings of *vikshepa* will drive their target (you) to believe that this spiral is a true sign of failure. But there's no reason to get disheartened. What we need to keep in mind is that the brain is an active, malleable organ, and that no matter how far we may feel from lined up, there is no failure as long as we continue to make an effort to realign. Further, willpower is like a muscle: it gets tired. Use and regular exercise—in the form of meditation and mindfulness—will strengthen it.

It is helpful to understand the qualities of practice as listed in sutra 1.13. Practice—in this case, the practice of realigning yourself back up the vibrational spectrum—must be consistent, executed over a long period of time, and done with passion.

When I was in the car, the GPS didn't say "Proceed to your destination and do it right now!" It didn't take control of the wheel and force me back onto the path. It simply stated "Please return to the highlighted route." It seemed to understand that sometimes there might be a few hundred miles between where the driver is and the destination. And maybe sometimes we veer off the path a bit. But as long as the driver is moving toward the route, the system settles down. And your emotions do that as well. In other words, you are not meant to define an idea and then manifest it instantaneously. You just want to get moving in the approximate direction of it because it turns out that *the true joy is in the journey*.

The true joy is in the journey? How can that be?

Say you decide to take a vacation. You make a plan with several destination spots along the way. You say, "Well, I'm going to stop here and here and here and here and here and eventually I'll go back home." Do you look at the trip you've planned and say "WAIT . . . all of those places, but the final destination is home? I'm already there . . . why go?"

You don't go on your vacation because you want to get it *done*. You go for the fun along the way, for inspiration, for interaction with new people and things, to expand yourself and your thoughts, to *LIVE*. And it's the same with everything else. With any destination—whether it's health, finances, love, or an actual trip—you are always in the process of further creation and it will always be that way. Such is the human experience.

> *When you set out on your journey to Ithaca,*
>
> *pray that the road is long,*
>
> *full of adventure, full of knowledge.*
>
> *The Lestrygonians and the Cyclops,*
>
> *the angry Poseidon—do not fear them:*
>
> *You will never find such as these on your path*
>
> *if your thoughts remain lofty, if a fine*
>
> *emotion touches your spirit and your body.*
>
> *The Lestrygonians and the Cyclops,*
>
> *the fierce Poseidon you will never encounter,*

if you do not carry them within your soul,

if your heart does not set them up before you.

Pray that the road is long.

That the summer mornings are many, when,

with such pleasure, with such joy

you will enter ports seen for the first time;

stop at Phoenician markets,

and purchase fine merchandise,

mother-of-pearl and coral, amber and ebony,

and sensual perfumes of all kinds,

as many sensual perfumes as you can;

visit many Egyptian cities,

to learn and learn from scholars.

Always keep Ithaca in your mind.

To arrive there is your ultimate goal.

But do not hurry the voyage at all.

It is better to let it last for many years;

and to anchor at the island when you are old,

rich with all you have gained on the way,

not expecting that Ithaca will offer you riches.

Ithaca has given you the beautiful voyage.

Without her you would never have set out on the road.

She has nothing more to give you.

And if you find her poor, Ithaca has not deceived you.

Wise as you have become, with so much experience,

you must already have understood what Ithaca means.

~ *Constantine Cavafy, "Ithaca"*

Translated by Rae Dalven

Vibing is the art of learning how—*by harnessing control of your thoughts so that you consciously align yourself on your path*—to soften your emotions little by little until you get in vibrational alignment with your own desires. And when you do that, the feeling is unbelievable! Even without the actual manifestation of the object of your desire. When you get in sync with the power of you—with your right and ability to create, then you can relax and acknowledge that there is nothing that you cannot be or do or have, *but you don't have to be or do or have it all right now.* There is plenty to enjoy in the present moment and plenty coming along the way.

So what are emotions? And why is it that they have such a huge impact on our ability or disability to stay on the path that we are choosing? We can understand our emotional nature and how it works by looking at the *koshas.*

The *koshas*, or sheaths, are representations of the different layers that we each have—energetic veils that cover our eternal, immortal, true selves and provide us with levels of experience as human beings. The *koshas* are enveloped within each other from the most subtle in nature to the grossest, much the same way that Russian nesting dolls are stacked one inside the next.

The physical body is known as the *Annamaya kosha* or food sheath, so called because the body is literally made up of the food that we eat.

> *From food are made all bodies, which become*
>
> *Food again for others after their death.*
>
> *Food is the most important of all things*
>
> *For the body; therefore it is the best*
>
> *Medicine for all the body's ailments.*
>
> *They who look upon food as the Lord's gift*
>
> *Shall never lack life's physical comforts.*
>
> *From food are made all bodies. All bodies*
>
> *Feed on food, and it feeds on all bodies. (Taittiriya Upanishad II.2.1)[18]*

The *koshas* provide different compartments or worlds that make up the domain of our experience as well as the path of spirituality through the practice of yoga, mindfulness, and meditation. We can see the *Annamaya kosha* as the densest of the layers. In an analogy, it is like a computer, devoid of any software and without the electrical circuit plugged in. The person stuck in the realm of the *Annamaya kosha* identifies solely and fully as nothing more than the physical body with all the limitations inherently implied within that finite concept of self. For them, there is nothing beyond this physical life.

---

18   Eknath Easwaran, *The Upanishads*, p. 145

The following *koshas* we can think of as different types of computer software running through the *Annamaya kosha*, giving us some real clues as to how thoughts and emotions restrict or help us on our path.

The *Pranamaya kosha* is the breath sheath, known as the vital or subtle body. We can all agree that without breath, we are nothing. What rides on the breath is equally important. Prana is life force energy, "pra" meaning "first" and "ana" meaning "to animate." It comes to us in a number of ways, but predominately as we breathe. If you have ever witnessed the passing of life from a living being, you have seen clearly that life essence (or spirit, or Soul) moves from the body on the final breath, leaving an empty vessel behind.

> *Man and woman, beast and bird live by breath.*
>
> *Breath is therefore called the true sign of life.*
>
> · *It is the vital force in everyone*
>
> *That determines how long we are to live.*
>
> *Those who look upon breath as the Lord's gift*
>
> *Shall live to complete the full span of life. (Taittiriya Upanishad II.3.1)*[19]

This is the energy that animates all beings from plants to people, and is the sheath through which we encounter feelings. This occurs primarily through the chakras and secondarily through the brain.

The word chakra means "wheel." The chakras are seven multidimensional wheels of energy through which we experience emotions. Chakras are the points where prana moves—in association with certain areas of the body—to be experienced as feelings:

- *Muladhara chakra* is located at the base of the spine; it governs the spectrum of experience from rootedness to fear

---

19   Eknath Easwaran, *The Upanishads*, p. 146

- *Svadisthana chakra* is located in the pelvic bowl; it governs the spectrum of experience from sensual exploration to lust and addiction

- *Manipura chakra* is located in the solar plexus; it governs the spectrum of experience from confidence to unworthiness and shame

- *Anahata chakra* is located in the heart and lungs; it governs the spectrum of experience from universal love to jealousy, grief, and isolation

- *Vishuddha chakra* is located in the throat; it governs the spectrum of experience from creativity to frustration

- *Ajna chakra* is located at the third eye point; it governs the spectrum of experience from clarity to confusion

- *Sahasrara chakra* is located at the crown of the head; it governs the spectrum of experience from divinity to distraction

Excess movement into the lower three chakras is responsible for feelings connected with our instinctual negative emotions, such as lust, fear, and egotism. Movement of vital energy into the higher chakras is connected with positive emotions. Through the process of meditation, we bring energy up through the central column of the spine (the *Sushumna Nadi*, or energetic superhighway) toward the upper chakras, and more positive emotion.

The word *manas* means "mind." The mind is located in the *Manomaya kosha* or mental sheath. This is the space of thought in the simplest of terms, receiving a stimulus and reacting to that stimulus. It is the *Manomaya kosha* that traps most people within the cycle of the reactive habits of thought, word, and deed that we know as *samskaras*. This is also the *kosha* through which we can begin to alter those patterns, first by recognizing them and then by taking steps to change them.

Realizing that from which all words turn back

And thoughts can never reach, one knows

The bliss of Brahman and fears no more. (Taittiriya Upanishad II.4.1)[20]

Within the *Manomaya kosha* is the limbic system, a complex network of nerves in the brain concerned with instinct and mood. This system controls the basic emotions (fear, pleasure, anger) and drives (hunger, sex, dominance, care for offspring), and is the seat of the value judgments that we make, often unconsciously, that exert such a strong influence on our behavior. It is here that we can start to do the work of looking at and refining our emotionally reactive tendencies.

In *My Stroke of Insight*, Jill Bolte Taylor discusses "response-ability," the ability to choose how we respond to stimulation coming in through our sensory systems at any moment in time. When we understand why we feel nervous, annoyed, hassled, driven, blue, or inadequate, those feelings have less power over us. How?

"Although there are certain limbic (emotional) programs that can be triggered automatically, it takes less than 90 seconds for one of these programs to be triggered, surge through our body, and then be completely flushed out of our bloodstream. Within 90 seconds from the initial trigger, the chemical or physiological component of the emotion has completely dissipated from the blood and the automatic response is over."[21]

Here's what's fascinating and fantastic: if the emotional condition remains after the ninety seconds has elapsed, it is because the person has chosen to let that circuit continue to run.

You are making your way, vibing along, when a feeling that doesn't feel so good presents itself. Doubt? Frustration? Anger? Whatever the emotional program is, physiologically it is going to run itself out within a minute and a half. That's it! If you can take that minute and a half to move back into the present moment, you will have successfully navigated yourself out of the downward spiral of *vikshepa*.

You will also have successfully navigated through the *Manomaya kosha* to the deeper, subtler realm of the *Vijnamaya kosha*.

---

20   Eknath Easwaran, *The Upanishads*, p. 143
21   Jill Bolte Taylor, *My Stroke of Insight*, p. 146

Within the mental sheath, made up of waves

Of thought, there is contained the sheath of wisdom.

It has the same form, with faith as the head,

Righteousness as right arm and truth as left

Practice of meditation is its heart,

And discrimination its foundation.

Wisdom means a life of selfless service.

Even the gods seek spiritual wisdom.

Those who attain wisdom are freed from sin,

And find all their selfless desires granted. (Taittiriya Upanishad 11.4.1)[22]

Vijnamaya kosha is the wisdom sheath, where we discriminate and act in a more thoughtful and objective manner. This is the space through which we develop the discipline of mindfulness in our daily lives, and move beyond our patterns of conditioning. It is through the *Vijnamaya kosha* that the blinders fall away, revealing signs that we are on the right path, the objectivity to see contrasting evidence as a way to gain further clarity, and opportunity toward that which we are looking to create.

The *Anandamaya kosha* is the bliss body, described by Sri Dharma Mittra as "the innermost and finest of all the Koshas (and that which is closest to the pure consciousness of Atman, the Higher Self). It is the causal body and permeates all the other koshas. The yogi who resides in the bliss sheath experiences absolute peace, joy and love. This bliss sheath offers a perfect reflection of Atman: a spontaneous and effortless joy that is independent of any reason or stimulus that may cause a mental reaction. The subtlest of the five koshas, the Anandamaya kosha is the layer of witness to the self in the silence of deep meditation."

22   Eknath Easwaran, *The Upanishads*, p. 146

And in the depth of his meditation

He created everything that exists.

Meditating, he entered into everything. (Taittiriya Upanishad II.6.6)[23]

When you learn to manage the vibrational relationship between where you are and where you want to be by understanding and working through the experiences of the *koshas*, life becomes sweet—even though your desires are not yet fulfilled.

I once had a conversation with a fellow viber who was really in a state of depression. Within five minutes of speaking with her, I realized that if I mentioned anything to her that even hinted at the statement *what you perceive you receive*, she would have either spontaneously combusted or ripped my head off. And there are things that she wants and is working toward manifesting in her life, but the feeling she was experiencing at that time was a clear indication that she was out of sync vibrationally. She had careened off her path.

Emotions are such a blessing, because they provide important information about the vibrational spectrum between the thoughts that you are thinking and what you really want to manifest.

Joseph Campbell offered an unbelievably powerful and yet simple statement when he said, "follow your bliss." But, like my depressed friend, sometimes it's downright impossible to get a whiff of bliss or belief because you have spiraled down the rabbit hole where bliss is impossible to find. But fear not! In those moments, when you recognize how far away you are from feeling good, you can take steps to work yourself back up.

How? By taking your yogi vitamins.

Sutra 1.20 teaches us that practice must be pursued with five qualities—*sraddha* (faith), *virya* (strength), *smriti* (memory), *prajnapurvaka* (discernment), and *samadhi* (absorption). These qualities are to be cultivated each and every day; in the same way that we take certain nutrients daily to make sure we are in optimal physical health.

---

23   Eknath Easwaran, *The Upanishads*, p. 147

Sraddha is faith, defined as complete trust or confidence. It is our ability to carry on when the going gets tough, knowing that the proverbial light is at the end of the tunnel, even during those times when we can't see the slightest glimmer.

> *When a person is devoted to something with complete faith, I unify his faith in that. Then, when his faith is completely unified, he gains the object of his devotion. In this way, every desire is fulfilled by me. (The Bhagavad Gita,* 7.21–7.23)[24]

Virya is the strength to stay on the path, to continue the practice of vibing no matter how much you feel that it may be time to give up. Strength is not something that develops on its own. The only way to develop strength is to develop strength! It is the same thing with vibing. We must cultivate the mental strength in every moment in order to line ourselves up with that which we are looking to create. And to that end, *smriti* (memory) and *prajnapurvaka* (discernment) can greatly aid us. When we look to our past conditioning and previous experiences in terms of what we are vibing on, those memories will provide one of two things. If what we are experiencing is in line with what we are looking to create, it will provide us with the support that we need to carry on. If not, then it provides *contrast* by showing us what we *don't* want so we can create what we *do* want. It is our ability to take a moment (and sometimes a few deep breaths) and discern what the emotions and thought patterns are providing us with. The ability to stay present and discriminating—especially in those times when the distractions seem to have us bound—is how we train ourselves time and again to take responsibility for our lives. And that is how we create.

The more we work with these four qualities, the more we are able to come back to a place of absorption with our vibe (*samadhi*). It may take some time. But remember, you only get the benefit of a vitamin by incorporating it consistently into your diet . . . yogi vitamins as well!

You can't get to the good stuff from the place of feeling bad. It simply doesn't work. But what is great and powerful and practical is the fact that you can soothe yourself by staying present with your thoughts and by actively looking for some that make you feel better emotionally. You can be in a place of despair or

---

24   Eknath Easwaran, *The Bhagavad Gita*, p. 144

depression and take teeny tiny steps to a place where you feel a little better . . . and a little better. And the more of those little steps you take, the more you:

1. Move back onto your path

2. Show yourself that you can actually take control of the way you feel

So, as an example, let's take my depressed friend. Imagine that she loves her job, but feels that she's getting more work and lacks the time to do it all. She's joined the Vibe-a-Thon with a desire to manifest a more easeful, flowing job situation, one that allows her time to breathe. She completed the first week's exercises and spent a blissful two or three days vibing and having fun with it, when suddenly . . . WHAM! Her boss comes into her office with five new projects, all of which she is solely responsible for and all of which need to be completed by the end of the week.

She is utterly depressed. "Woe is me" is her new mantra. She feels defeated, as though she'll never be able to have the work situation that she wants.

Now, let's say that she has done a good job with her exercises and meditation to date. Therefore, she recognizes that she is starting to spiral away from the vibing she has done and into the distractions. She feels the doubt, as well as the inherent laziness that takes the form of "Why bother?" Instead of moving more deeply into a free fall toward despondency, she takes a moment and closes her eyes. It's challenging for her to get to a place where she feels good and hope-ful about her current situation, so instead she takes a few breaths and tries to dig up a memory of the times when things have seemed dark but then worked out in the end. At first the memories don't come so quickly, but with a bit of time and patience she discerns the thoughts that show her evidence, helping to soothe the anxiety that she was feeling strongly moments ago. She knows that emotional reactions run a physiological response through the body that takes around a minute and a half to complete. After that, it's her choice whether or not to loop through the reactive cycle again. She wisely chooses not to, by continuing to breathe deeply and to soothe herself with the good memories. As she softens a bit more, she comes to a calmer, more open place where maybe she doesn't feel a full-blown explosion of faith that things will work out as she wants, but a little bit of a spark. She understands that perhaps there is a bit of conditioning from her past preventing her from lining up at the moment. Moreover, this current experience is in reality not bad at all, for it is showing her the contrast of what she doesn't want in order for her to gain more clarity on exactly what she does want.

She moves through the rest of her day much less affected by her current workload, focused more on how powerful and proud she feels in her ability to actively create her day, instead of reacting to something that in the end is merely contrast that will more specifically help her craft what she is looking to create. Before she knows it, she is faithful that she can have the work situation that she wants. And now, she's back on her path. She has reoriented herself on her vibrational spectrum.

See how it can work? If you can start *soothing* yourself when you don't feel so great emotionally—by making conscious choices about how you feel, no matter how small a step it may seem—then you will have begun using probably the most effective, important tool helping you create your life. And it may be as simple as saying to yourself *OK, so I don't feel so lined up right now. So what? I'll get there . . .*

Because you will. Remember: it's an internal, mindful *journey*. And the path from where you are to where you want to be has bumps and diversions along the way. But you've got your emotions to guide you. And the divergent thoughts are the tools with which we teach ourselves how to think and feel our way back up to alignment. What more do you need?

> *This being human is a guest house.*
>
> *Every morning a new arrival.*
>
>
> *A joy, a depression, a meanness,*
>
> *some momentary awareness comes as an*
>
> *unexpected visitor.*

Welcome and entertain them all!

Even if they're a crowd of sorrows,

who violently sweep your house empty of its furniture,

still, treat each guest honorably.

He may be clearing you out

for some new delight.

The dark thought, the shame, the malice

meet them at the door laughing,

and invite them in.

Be grateful for whoever comes,

because each has been sent

as a guide from beyond.

~ Rumi, "The Guest House"

Exercises for Week Two

Exercise #1: Journaling through the emotional process

Write a dialogue, expressing how you feel with respect to an aspect or event in your life that's not going quite as well as you'd like it to go. Get descriptive with it—any outside factors that may be a part of the cause (i.e., other people, the weather, life, etc.) as well as any action by you that may have added to the situation. *The subject of this exercise should **not** be the subject of your Vibe-a-Thon!*

Keep writing, but as you do, begin to soothe yourself and to soften the statements. The exercise is working if you feel better and better about the subject as you write. Keep going until you feel you have reached a place of clarity and alignment. (If you need an example, reread the paragraphs about the depressed friend as she soothed herself about the job situation, p. 102)

Remember: there is no right or wrong here, and there is no specific lineup of emotions you need to go through. Take time and soften the statements little by little.

Exercise #2: Clearing emotions attached to the subject of your Vibe-a-Thon

Take a look at the subject of your Vibe-a-Thon. Are there any negative emotions getting in the way of lining up with what you want? If so, repeat this week's first exercise, beginning your dialogue at the point on the vibrational spectrum you are *currently* experiencing.

Exercise #3: Daily emotional housekeeping

During the week, pay attention to your emotional guidance in your day-to-day life. As the normal emotional responses appear, make a conscious effort to soften and pacify the thoughts that aren't serving you, step by step. Remember, the physiological response you feel in your body as the effect of a thought or emotion has only a ninety second shelf life. Once it has run its "program," it's complete—unless you allow the pattern to perpetuate by continuing to react. To retrain yourself in a way that is in line with the new, vibing you:

- Take a deep breath (or ten or twenty), focusing more on the exhale than the inhale. (In moments of stress, we tend to inhale more than we exhale. In so doing, we risk hyperventilating ourselves.)

- From this (hopefully) calmer place, identify exactly what the emotion is that you are feeling. Does it have a physical representation in the body? Exactly where are you feeling it . . . and what does it feel like? For example, maybe it's a hardening in the pit of your stomach, which you could represent as an iron ball.

- As you continue to quiet your mind and focus on the breath, with each exhale move the image that you've created farther and farther down your body, through your feet and to the core of the earth.

As you do this, acknowledge the fact that you're making yourself feel better. Practice makes perfect, and the more you work with internal guidance in your daily life, the easier it will be to use it for the more daunting things.

Meditation: The Session

1. 5 minutes—Alternate Nostril Breathing (i.e., *Nadi Shodhana*)

2. 3 minutes—Breath Awareness

3. 7–10 minutes—Effortful Concentration (*Dharana*)

   a. Bring your attention to a point of focus inside of yourself—anything you choose is fine. The Ajna chakra (the third eye point) or the Anahata chakra (the heart) are often used.

   b. Keep your internal gaze softly focused there. When thoughts come up, don't judge or analyze. Just bring yourself back to the point of focus. Note that emotions can have a profoundly distracting effect on our ability to focus in meditation.

However, they are often the residue of something (or things) that no longer serve you (in terms of contrast) and are ready to be released. If you find that a particular emotion comes up, try to allow it in without attaching any identifying labels to it. For example, if anger starts to well up, *resist the urge to figure out what you are angry about.* Simply sit with the anger. As you do—again, without attaching to or labeling it—the emotion softens and eventually disappears.

4.   5 minutes—Visualization

Supplemental information, support and community for vibers can be found online at www.vibeathon.com.

Remember, what you perceive you receive ... Now, vibe on to week two!

Day Nine: C'mon . . . Get Happy!

Enjoy your life and be happy.

Being happy is of the utmost importance.

Success in anything is through happiness.

More support of nature comes from being happy.

Under all circumstances be happy, even if you have to force it a bit to change some long-standing habits. Just think of any negativity that comes to you as a raindrop falling into the ocean of your bliss.

You may not always have an ocean of bliss, but think that way anyway and it will help it come. Doubting is not blissful and does not create happiness. Be happy, healthy, and let all that love flow through your heart.

~ Maharishi Mahesh Yogi

Presence and contentment in the moment take care of so much! They allow us to line up vibrationally and they bring into life all the wonderful things that we're looking for, because in happiness there is great opening and less resistance. And from such a place comes allowing, so things can present in the field of perception . . . and, therefore, become reality.

But what about those days when you feel like you have absolutely no reason to be content? To help bring yourself back into alignment, practice a bit of *pratipaksha bhavanam.*

Pratipaksha bhavanam? What the heck is that?

Pratipaksha bhavanam is the practice of forming opposite thoughts when disturbed by negative ones. We know that negative thoughts are those that bring us out of

alignment with what we are trying to vibe on. If we attempt to let go of the negative thoughts or to suppress them, quite often those thoughts come exploding back
with more vengeance than they had the first time the thought occurred. There is a
simple reason for this: in striving to prevent or push down those negative thoughts,
what we are actually doing on a subconscious level is activating more and more
focus on that thought. Have you ever decided to "give up" something in the morning, only to find that by the end of the day you have brought yourself full on into the
exact experience in a way that was stronger than ever before?

If we work instead at replacing negative thoughts with their opposite, positive
counterparts, we can bring ourselves back into vibrational alignment. It's a
practice for sure, but one that will both keep you on your path and in a more
open, constructive place going forward.

Pratipaksha bhavanam is directly applicable to the internal journey that we have
undertaken. If we are in a place of thinking something is impossible and can get
to a thought of it being totally possible, then great! And in those moments when
going from impossible to possible seems *impossible*, *pratipaksha bhavanam* can still
work. We can discern a thought that's a little better . . . and a little better . . .
bringing ourselves back up the emotional scale until we feel lined up again.

If you feel you have absolutely no reason to be happy, try to imagine moving
in a positive direction and go along for the ride. This often requires a decision
that you are going to be happy by whatever means necessary, and then identifying the stimulus that elicits any type of negatively reactive pattern inside of
you so you can direct the thought elsewhere and soften the internal and/or
external response. The "noise" out in the world in the form of media and social
networking—as well as the noise in our own environmental circles— is fertile
ground for the work of *pratipaksha bhavanam*.

We hold the keys to manifestation by keeping ourselves calm, peaceful, and
open. But what about the reactive patterns that we have toward other people?
You know, the person who consistently rubs you the wrong way? The friend
who, by sharing good news, triggers that evil green monster of jealousy that
we hate to admit we experience but that often puts vibing into a tailspin?

The Sutras have it covered . . . again! In one of the most beloved of all the sutras, 1.33, Patanjali states that we can come to a place of peace in our minds by cultivating an attitude of friendliness toward the happy, compassion for the unhappy, delight in the virtuous, and equanimity when faced with those whose actions oppose our values. Fantastic! Let's look at each one of these "keys" and explore how they specifically release us from the judgments and perceptions that keep us away from the infinite abundance that is truly available for all.

Friendliness / kindness toward those who are happy

> *If I said as sunnily as I could, "Hey, Mrs. Dubose," I would receive for an answer, "Don't you say hey to me, you ugly girl! You say good afternoon, Mrs. Dubose!"*
>
> *~ Harper Lee, To Kill a Mockingbird*

Sometimes the happiness of other people can trigger our own feelings of lack or unfulfilled desire. The unsubstantiated belief that there is only a certain amount of happiness, love, joy, or even stuff can keep us focused on what *they* have created as evidence that *we* have somehow failed. Nonsense! By cultivating an attitude of friendliness toward the happy, we can open our perceptions to the understanding that there is abundance for all, and use the example of others' happiness to inspire us instead of allowing it to contain us in a limited perspective. Why not look to the happiness of others as evidence that we are lining up more and more, and that the walls of perception are beginning to open wide?

We can turn the cultivation of that attitude toward ourselves as well. In the past, have you had the experience of sabotaging *yourself* when good things start to come in? Softening the judgment and criticism that often occurs inside of us a thousandfold more than externally can go a long way toward setting us on the path.

Friendliness toward those who are happy is the key to undisturbed calmness and the knowledge that there is abundance for all.

Compassion for those who are less fortunate

You never really understand a person until you consider things from his point of view . . . 'til you climb inside his skin and walk around in it.

~ *Harper Lee,* To Kill a Mockingbird

Disapproval and faultfinding with respect to those we deem as unhappy or less fortunate is an easy pattern of conditioning to repeat over and over again. Lack of compassion is often the effect of our own subconscious fears and anxiety about potential loss of control or inability to carry on under less than desirable circumstances. We can soften the judgment toward others by remembering that every living being is, at the core, the same divine, eternal life/God/Source/purity. And all of those radiant souls are covered in the conditioning and experiences in life that have brought them to their current challenge. Further, as there can be no light without the contrast of darkness, so too will we all go through our dark times. The ability to cultivate compassion for others can soften and open us up to developing compassion for ourselves when the challenges come.

Compassion is the key to acceptance and provides the contrast necessary for fine-tuning our own vibe.

Delight in the virtuous

It was a sin to kill a mockingbird. Why? Well, I reckon because mockingbirds don't do anything but make music for us to enjoy. They don't eat people's gardens, don't nest in the corncrib, they don't do one thing but just sing their hearts out for us.

~ *Harper Lee,* To Kill a Mockingbird

Why do we knock down those who do good? Often, because their goodness has the effect of showing us where we are lacking. Remember, human beings are hardwired for survival. For this reason, we have a strong tendency toward negativity, especially when we witness a virtuous person or deed. It's as though they have received a gold star in the survival of the fittest. What does that say about us?

By cultivating delight in the virtuous, we can stop taking people down because of insecurity resulting from fear that we are limited in *our* ability to create what we desire. In doing so, we find the key to uncovering positive evidence, inspiration, and encouragement to keep us on our path.

Delight in the virtuous is the key to rooting out evidence that we are on the path of our choosing.

Equanimity when faced with those whose actions oppose your values

> **There's a lot of ugly things in this world, son. I wish I could keep 'em all away from you. That's not possible.**
>
> ~ *Harper Lee*, To Kill a Mockingbird

What a great world it would be if we all acted in open, peaceful, loving ways toward each other. Unfortunately, that is not always the case. There are times when we see clearly that the actions of others truly are not in line with who we are, who we are becoming, and what we are trying to create in our lives. And though we try to show compassion to those people, it is clear that their attitudes or actions are creating stress in our experience as well as pain and confusion in our minds.

Equanimity when faced with those whose actions oppose your values is the key. Nothing is more important than your peaceful and open mind and heart to create that which you desire. It's as simple as that. Do what you can to soften the effect of their actions by staying levelheaded and calm within yourself.

Equanimity is the key to moving beyond those challenges that seem hard to navigate.

Just remember: nothing is more important than giving priority to your mental and spiritual health. So get yourself happy!

For Today:

1.   Continue with meditation.

2. For consideration: During the day, pay particular attention to the thoughts and feelings that come up in reaction to the people, experiences, and ideas that are brought into your field of perception. Can you soften those reactive tendencies through the use of *pratipaksha bhavanam* and/or by cultivating attitudes of friendliness toward the happy, compassion for the less fortunate, delight in the virtuous, and equanimity when faced with those whose actions oppose your values? If you find it challenging to do this simply through a thought process, try journaling.

Supplemental information, support and community for vibers can be found online at www.vibeathon.com.

Remember, what you perceive you receive . . . Now, vibe on!

Day Ten: The Brilliance of Animals and the Eight Limbs of Yoga

I was in my apartment one day, diligently thinking about what to send out to the participants in the first Vibe-a-Thon. Thinking, thinking . . . thinking. As I was thinking, my cat, Wilma, came and sat on my lap. She does this whenever she's ready to be petted. Because when I pet her, she feels good. That's the wonderful thing about animals. They love to feel good and they spend their lives in that pursuit.

So, as I sat with her on my lap—thinking . . . thinking . . . thinking—I realized that she was sitting and waiting . . . waiting . . . waiting. She had her vibration set to feeling good, and as she held her gaze at me there was no blinking, no wavering. She was completely confident that if she focused her attention on what she wanted long enough, eventually it would become manifest. And you know what? It worked. Within a minute or so, I was petting her and she was purring.

Almost the same thing happened a few hours later as I worked with a client who had a dog. Every time I went to this client's home, the dog greeted me by eagerly running over with one of her toys, dropping it in the most accessible spot for me to pick up and toss. And she sat . . . and stared . . . and waited.

We can look to the single-mindedness of these animals as an example of the experiential states that are available to us as we deepen our practice of yoga. As both pets waited patiently for their desire to become reality, it was easy to see that their concentration was keenly focused on one point without wavering. Further, when an animal is in that state of one-pointed focus, its body, mind, and spirit are totally absorbed in the moment, ready for what's to come next. Absolute, utter concentration almost comes more naturally to animals than it does to us. How easy would it be for us to vibe and create what we desire in life if we could harness our attention in the way that our pets can channel theirs?

While our minds are larger, more complex, and inherently more scattered than animals', our capacity to concentrate can be exercised and strengthened through the practices offered in the eight limbs, or *ashtanga yoga*, delineated by Patanjali.

Within the second book of the Yoga Sutras, the Sadhana Pada or portion on practice, Patanjali offers a clear system to lead us from activity in the world to the experience of Oneness within. By consistently cultivating each of the eight steps, we heighten our ability to focus attention in all aspects of our lives.

The first three limbs are external and physical in nature. *Yamas*, our external ethical principles, include *ahimsa* (non-violence), *satya* (truthfulness), *asteya* (non-stealing), *brahmacharya* (moderation), and *aparigraha* (non-greed). In the same way that a little bit of residue from kerosene can block the flame inside a lantern from view, even the smaller deviations away from these practices can keep us from clarity in our minds and hearts. And yet, the sutras related to the *yamas* clearly show the great gifts that stem from their practice:

2.35. *In the presence of one firmly established in non-violence, all hostilities cease.*

2.36. *The words of one established in truthfulness become so potent that whatever he says comes to realization.*

2.37. *To one established in non-stealing, all wealth comes.*

2.38. *Vigor is gained by one established in moderation.*

2.39. *One established in non-greed gains the ability to see how his desires affect what he experiences in life*

The *niyamas* are our individual ethical principles, including *saucha* (purity), *samtosha* (contentment), *tapas* (withstanding intensity for its power of transformation, see day seven), *svadhyaya* (self-study), and *Isvarapranidhana* (surrender to God or to something beyond oneself). In practicing *saucha*, we take care of our bodies: internally by means of the things we ingest and externally through the activities we do to keep our bodies both healthy and clean. *Samtosha* means contentment, and is the practice of maintaining an emotional neutrality or coolness at all times. This can often be misconstrued as dispassion or happiness, though neither is the case. Dispassion can be felt as disconnection, whereas in contentment there is absolute presence. Happiness has an emotional charge that, to a positive degree, can deliver the same wallop to the nervous system as depression. Contentment is our ability to be OK with what is. The last three *niyamas* constitute the tenets of *kriya yoga*, and provide us with tools to stay actively present and mindful in daily life.

Asana, posture, is possibly the most misunderstood of all the limbs, the one that modern Western culture has taken and run with, often to the exclusion of yoga's more intrinsic and important practices. And that's OK, because when correctly taught the physical practice that most know as yoga has tremendous benefit for the body, mind, and spirit and can be an effective tool for training the mind to focus. However, as used in the context of the eight limbs, asana is nothing more than the posture we sit in for meditation. The postures we identify as "yoga" were developed because sadhus (practitioners) found it challenging to sit for long periods of time in meditation owing to corporal aches and creaks and to digestive upsets. So we can look at asana as how we sit when getting ready for meditation.

The next two limbs are internal in nature. After opening and preparing the body physically through asana (which—when done with focus—has a calming effect on the mind), we are primed to work with the breath. *Pranayama* is the practice of directing and controlling the flow of breath in and out of the body. In doing so, the distractions begin to drift away as we focus within, further calming the emotions and drawing our attention away from habitually reactive thoughts. Through *pratyahara* we draw the senses inward, away from external reaching and toward the more subtle realms.

These first five limbs are the active practice and lead to the final three limbs. The last three limbs form *samyama yoga*. *Samyama* encompasses the experiential states wherein we come to a place of Oneness with our true nature or Soul, and where the walls that limit our perception fall away. *Dharana* is effortful concentration, the state where we do the work of binding the mind to one place, object, or idea. As you undoubtedly know by now, the mind is not in the habit of staying fixed on any one point, but wants to dart all over. We can think that we are focused and yet somehow find that we are totally lost in a daydream. This is where effort must come into play. Over time, as we train the mind, it becomes more still and focused on our point of attention. This is a vital tool for vibing. *Dhyana* is the experiential state of continuous flow of cognition toward the point of focus. Hindu scriptures give a beautiful example: they compare this to pouring oil from one pot to another. It is a continuous string that does not break. When we are totally at one with our point of focus, no other thoughts intrude. We are solidly connected with the place, object, or idea and the struggle to keep our attention there is alleviated. As we move more deeply in, fully absorbed and beyond labels and identifications, we come to a place of communion with all living things and with God. That state is *samadhi*. "When you have realized this prolonging of the tranquil state where the rising thoughts and the restrained thoughts come to an end, at the culmination of the process of stilling the rising and restrained thoughts, the consciousness and intelligence are drawn as if by a magnet towards the core of the being. To live in totality with your energy, your intelligence and your consciousness as one single unit, knotted to the core of the being, is meditation."[25]

The hopeful, patient, knowing expectation and concentration that we witness in animals is available to us as well. It takes longer and requires more effort to get to it because our thinking minds are in the way, but through working with the limbs of *ashtanga yoga* and continuing to do the work of meditation and mindfulness in your daily life, the walls of perception will begin to open. And then, more and more, you will experience evidence of and opportunity for the things that you are looking to create in your life.

For Today:

1. Continue with meditation, paying particular attention to the process of drawing your attention back to the point of focus when you find it has moved away (*dharana*). With time, you will create a greater capacity to dwell in the space that exists between resting in a place of concentration and moving out to a thought. As this amount of time deepens, you will spend more time experiencing the state of meditation (*dhyana*).

2. For consideration: Choose one of the five *yamas* (non-violence, truthfulness, non-stealing, moderation, non-greed). During the course of your day, make an active practice of that *yama*. How does it feel? How

---

25   B. K. S. Iyengar, *The Tree of Yoga*, p. 145

does it help you in continuing to line up with what you are looking to create?

Supplemental information, support and community for vibers can be found online at www.vibeathon.com.

Remember, what you perceive you receive . . . Now, vibe on!

Day Eleven: The Active, Nonreactive, Choice-Based Life

The only way to predict the future is to create it.

Life is not fate. There is nothing predetermined about it. Life is the culmination of the myriad of choices that we have made—and continue to make—through the course of every moment of this existence.

A choice is presented to you. And from the possibilities, you choose. From that choice comes a consequence. Good, bad, or otherwise, because of the choice that you made, something happened. And now, from this consequence comes a new set of choices. Once again, you choose. And so on and so forth.

I know in theory this seems logical. But what about those times when things happen *to* us? What then?

Even in the more challenging situations when we feel that we are struggling with the quagmire that arises from the consequences of someone else's choice(s), we must open up to the consideration that to some lesser or greater extent, we were coparticipants in creating what might appear as the result of someone else's actions. Perhaps we participated in cocreating passively, by turning a blind eye to a situation until it spiraled out of control or maybe we subconsciously entered into an argument because it was the habitual response to do so. It may have been a situation that we should have stepped out of long ago. The vast majority of consequences that we come up against in our lives are of our own doing.

How wonderful!

Wonderful? Huh?

In every moment, we have choice. And so, the more present, mindful, and conscious we become, the more actively (and, therefore, less *reactively*) we are able to choose. When we are presented with a situation that habitually presses the button to a particular reaction, instead of automatically playing that reactive tape out, we can now actively choose what is in line with who we truly are and what we are working to create in our lives.

Soooo . . . if you have been unconsciously supporting and strengthening a reactive *samskara* for a long time, does it mean that it will take an equally long period of time to change that pattern? No! The reactive pattern was both created and reinforced subconsciously. You basically let your mind run amok, and the inmates (your thoughts) have been running the asylum. Changing the pattern can be relatively easy once you make an active, conscious choice to do so. But remember, this is a process. You need to be diligent, consistent, and patient with yourself. Thought processes dominate our lives, but not in directed thinking. Most thought impressions are the result of undisciplined thinking; they are associated with memories and with the reactive tapes that are so easily triggered. Repatterning is even more challenging because of the negativity bias that has allowed the human species to evolve through survival of the fittest. We need to keep in mind that our choices are quite often an attempt at resisting something negative as opposed to reaching for something positive.

Oy! We definitely have our work cut out for us! The amount of time it takes for you to reprogram the reactive thought patterns and conditioned responses will directly correlate to the amount of conscious attention you bring to changing them.

In sutra 1.13, we learn that practice is a steadfast effort to calm the mind. But we have to recognize that the work of daily meditation is not enough, that it is in the world that we play in *after* sitting where the thoughts will wreak the most havoc. And so practice must incorporate the application of mindfulness in every moment. It is arduous work in the beginning for sure, and as with everything the goal is near for those who are vigorous and intense in practice, as stated in sutra 1.21. Sutra 1.22 shows us that the time necessary for success depends on whether the practice is mild, medium, or intense. Success will come, but only to the extent that you take on the work.

Meditation is the process of clearing the clutter in our minds. In the introduction we looked at the mind as a room that you would like to redesign. The room is filled with so much stuff that you can't get a clear sense of the amount of space you have to work with: how the light plays in the room, how you would like to rework the things that you own within the space, and what new objects you might like to bring in.

The first thing you need to do is clear out the room, in the same way that we first clear the mind through meditation. Then, through the process of staying diligently mindful outside of meditation, we discern the thoughts that are in line with what we are actively creating, and stay away from the reactive patterns that no longer serve us—in the same way that Aunt Gladys's Civil War–inspired wall hanging may no longer suit the room you redecorate.

We are conditioned beings. Deep inside, we share the internal, immortal light that connects us all and lives within the field of infinite possibility. Covering that luminosity are all of our individual experiences and conditioning, along with layers of societal conditioning and beliefs. Our work is to look within; to get to that infinite space inside; to use the experience of that peace and space and take a moment before we react; to take a breath, discern what our reaction could be, and to make a conscious, active choice that is in line with the direction we want to go in.

Today is the day to stop living reactively and to start actively creating that which we are looking for. For when we react, we are living fully within the limited field of our previous conditioning and experiences, and those blinders prohibit us from opening up. When we discern and actively choose, the infinite field of possibilities opens to us, and life is there for the choosing.

Walking through Central Park one morning, I passed a small boy crying to his mother and on the verge of a full-blown meltdown. From what I could gather, the little boy's brother had possession of their basketball and had run ahead toward the playground. And then the most wonderful thing happened! No, no, he didn't throw himself prostrate on the ground with limbs a-flailing. The mother calmly told her son that he would get the ball as soon as they reached the playground—but only if he stopped crying.

The second after his mother spoke, this magnificent boy weepily replied "OK," stopped crying, and ran off to join his brother. What a beautiful reminder of how we are not bound to our reactions when we stay focused on what we truly want!

For Today:

1. Continue with meditation.

2. For consideration: Take some time during the course of the day and notice when the reactive patterns come up. Is there a particular set of circumstances that fosters a specific reaction for you? Reactions can be big or small and trigger physiological responses that only last ninety seconds unless we consciously or unconsciously reactivate them. When you feel something come up, take a deep breath (or ten or twenty) and start to repattern that *samskara*. It takes time, but you've got to start somewhere!

Supplemental information, support and community for vibers can be found online at www.vibeathon.com.

Remember, what you perceive you receive . . . Now, vibe on!

Day Twelve: It's Essence-ial

Faith is taking the first step, even when you don't see the full staircase.

~ Dr. Martin Luther King Jr.

Leslie is having a hard time holding her vision . . . because she doesn't have one. Nothing specific, at least. Her longtime career now leaves her joyless. She's burnt out, and wants fulfilling work that doesn't deplete her. And yet, she doesn't know what that new career is. Since she isn't vibing on anything specific, she is having a hard time holding on.

David is looking for love. A few women have crossed his path, but he finds that in each circumstance he feels pressured to adapt the qualities that he is vibing on to the woman—whether they fit or not. And so each woman becomes the "face" that will hopefully absorb what he is looking for, which is making him feel like he's living in a dream world because he's imposing characteristics on a person who may not have them.

Different situations, but by switching the focus slightly they will both be back on track. In both circumstances, our fellow vibers need to redirect their aware-ness back to the *essence* of what it is that they're trying to achieve. By doing so, they take the emphasis off what someone or something external will provide, and return the focus back where it belongs . . . on THEMSELVES. Because it is the perception that will change reality, and that happens from within.

Our human experience is a combination of matter and our internal processes that create our perception of that matter. As we know, our perception is the combined effect of a lifetime of conditioning, experiences, and our trained responses to those experiences. We can understand this a bit more deeply, first through psychology and then from the standpoint of the philosophy of yoga.

Carl Jung averred that, apart from the external senses, there are also discern-ible internal aspects of our conscious experience consisting of thinking, feeling, and intuiting.

What exactly do we think? The mind is what processes thought and meaning, not the brain, in the same way that a computer can sort through a series of inputs but cannot produce an emotional response to the information.

What do we feel? We feel energy-like movements that material instruments cannot directly measure, also known as prana in yoga and chi in Traditional Chinese Medicine (TCM). The concept of energy is one that cannot be explained by theories of conventional Western medicine, which can make it challenging for Western cultures to accept.

What do we intuit? In those moments when we are not caught in thoughts the dimension of intuitive experience opens up, offering archetypal or primal representations of concepts we value most, such as truth, beauty, love, goodness, etc. We call certain thoughts intuition because there is no rational explanation for them—they are outside of the realms of conditioning and experience that we relate to habitually. And this is magnificent, because when we get to that most subtle of places, we let go of the recurrent tapes that keep us limited and we open the parameters of our perception. The blinders have peeled away to expose us to new possibilities apart from the limiting qualifications that kept us from seeing beyond our current reality.

Quantum physics can be thought of as the science of infinite possibility and we, the observer or participant, choose from all possibilities the actual event of our experience. This is known as downward causation. As we saw earlier (see day three), downward causation posits that consciousness is the ground of all being; it asserts that we choose from the wide-open field of possibilities associated with a thought and that that thought eventually comes to actuality. When we are able to line ourselves up with the more subtle representations of what we are trying to create, the ego loosens up. The blinders begin to ease back, possibly opening us to new ideas and ways of thinking that will lead us to what will undoubtedly feel like new, fresh territory. And you take action from there. Remember, this starts with the work of the mind. The clearer you are up there—and the less you try to control the circumstances of how your vibe will play out—the more easily things will fall into place in your life.

One of the more challenging aspects of vibing is holding the vision of what we wish to create, without getting caught up in the details of how or when or where it will play out in our reality. And our egos have a really, really hard time adjusting to the idea that in order to open our fields of perception, we have to let go of our control and release the habitual thoughts that stand in our way. Quite simply, since the ego defines itself by its identifications (*I'm good at this*; *I'm lousy at this*), it really has no designs on opening up to possibilities beyond its labels.

Our intuition is the subtlest of our experiences. And so, the more we can get to the calm, quiet aspects of the mind, the more we can access that subtlety. By spending time in the practice of meditation, creating clarity in the mind, and easing the blinders off little by little, an organic process of opening happens. We become more aligned with the essence of what we are looking for, which creates freedom. And then we begin to experience new evidence of and opportunity for the creation of what we desire, which often happens in ways that we never expect. Why? Because our previous habits of thought and conditioning had kept us from seeing beyond the parameters they previously created.

> *May we light the fire of Nachiketa*
>
> *That burns out the ego and enables us*
>
> *To pass from fearful fragmentation*
>
> *To fearless fullness in the changeless whole. (Katha Upanishad III.2)*[26]

So, in the case of Leslie, instead of trying to figure out what she wants to do, she can focus on how great she will feel when she has the perfect career. She can vibe on waking up in the morning, excited and raring to go . . . the feeling of energy and stimulation through the course of the day . . . and the sense of accomplishment at the end of the day. David can imagine his life with the perfect relationship in it: how life will feel to be with an amazing woman, in true partnership with someone without limit or hesitation.

If they can hold on to their visions, do the work and *not get caught up in the details*, they will find that they are on the path sooner than they thought possible, and in the most entertaining of ways.

---

26   Eknath Easwaran, *The Upanishads*, p. 88

. . . and calleth those things that are not as though they were.

~ Romans 4:17

For Today:

1. Continue with meditation.

2. For consideration: Are you getting caught up in the details? Take a look at how you are vibing during the course of the day. Is it an open feeling of excitement that is lined up with the essence of what you want outside of the laundry list of qualifications . . . or are you getting a little too wrapped up in how you feel it should come to pass?

Supplemental information, support and community for vibers can be found online at www.vibeathon.com.

Remember, what you perceive you receive . . . Now, vibe on!

Day Thirteen: Stop Arguing!

Here's a question: Are you lining up with what you want to create or arguing for your limitations?

Sasha is working on lining up with her vision of having the home of her dreams. Every morning before coffee and the rest of the day, she practices meditation to clear her mind. During the last few minutes, she forms a vision of what the home will look like—and, more important, how it will feel to be in this lovely, lovely place. In that time, she comes to a space of confidence and knowing that she is on her way to where she wants to be.

But the day progresses and Sasha starts to question herself. She tries to get back to her vision, but instead of working through the contrast that could bring her more clarity on what she wants, she falls victim to the negative spiral. Statements such as *My credit is bad, there's no way I'm going to get a mortgage*; *I've never owned anything that big*; *Seriously, how can I handle that much responsibility* and *Why can't I just win the lottery so I can have exactly what I want?* run a vicious cycle through her mind.

Do you see how, by *arguing for her limitations*, Sasha is actually lining up with *not* having the home of her dreams? That, in actuality, she's pushing against what she really wants (beautiful home) and instead sending out a vibration of *lack*? And here's the interesting thing: we're not talking about anything other than how Sasha is thinking. She's keeping herself in a state of agitation, negativity, and confusion with her thoughts, instead of a peaceful, good-feeling place that comes when she lines up. And when she continues to argue for her limitations, those blinders on her field of perception stay firmly in place, providing ample evidence to support her disallowing belief and opportunity to firmly cement the resultant perspective as reality.

Why do we do that to ourselves? It happens all the time. We deal with it in our individual experience as well as in society, which often reinforces or informs our individual experience.

Throughout history, book burning has been a strategy used by people in power to silence opposing views. Over and over, we see how pushing against something (i.e., the ideas of one person) can actually proliferate that thing within the society that is pushing against it. Some examples:

- In the 1500s Catholic leaders torched the writings of Protestant reformer Martin Luther . . . and in so doing, inspired the rebellion of hundreds of thousands of people away from the Catholic Church and into the stream of alternative religious practices that were created during the Reformation.

- In 1881, when Boston's district attorney threatened to ban *Leaves of Grass*, the public went crazy for it. The profits paid for Walt Whitman's house.

- In 1939 copies of John Steinbeck's landmark novel, *The Grapes of Wrath*, were burned all over the country. Denigrators objected to Steinbeck's book about the tragic plight of migrant farm workers from the Oklahoma dust bowl for both its political content and "vulgarity." The book is today considered a literary classic.

Like focusing on an optical illusion, the more we draw attention to the negative, the more strongly we perceive evidence of and opportunity for it. And then we stay in the cycle of creating what we don't want instead of what we desire.

In sutra 2.16 Patanjali states *Heyam duhkham anagatam*, the pain that has not yet come is avoidable. This concept leads us to the contemplation of karma, meaning action and/or the result of action. There are three kinds of karma: the karma created in the past and leading to the present moment, the karma being expressed now, and the new karmas being created through our daily actions. We can't do anything about the first two karmas, as they represent both the energy already created and the multifaceted environment that we are presently in. But the karma that we create *now* can be fostered by staying mindful and by consciously cultivating thought patterns that are in line with what we wish to create. Our work with karma in our daily, present lives will determine our experiences of peace or sorrow, success or failure. This is what Patanjali means when he says that pain that has not yet come is avoidable. Today is the day to stop arguing for your limitations. It is absolutely within your right as a living being to create outside the parameters that previously confined you. By establishing the idea of what you desire in the Vibe-a-Thon, you planted the seed.

Now you fertilize the soil through meditation and further cultivate your crops by weeding out the limiting thoughts so that your crops can continue to bloom and flourish. Let your garden grow!

You carry

All the ingredients

To turn your life into a nightmare—

Don't mix them!

You have all the genius

To build a swing in your backyard

For God.

That sounds

Like a hell of a lot more fun.

Let's start laughing, drawing blueprints,

Gathering our talented friends.

I will help you

With my divine lyre and drum.

Hafiz

Will sing a thousand words

You take into your hands,

Like golden saws,

Silver hammers,

Polished teakwood,

Strong silk rope

You carry all the ingredients

To turn your existence into joy.

Mix them, mix

Them!

~ Hafiz, "To Build a Swing"[27]

For Today:

1. Continue with meditation.

2. For consideration: Stay mindful during the day and notice if and when you find that you argue for your limitations. Keep it outside the realm of your Vibe-a-Thon at first . . . you may be surprised at how easily you talk yourself out of something before you've even given it half a chance! From there, come to the subject of your Vibe-a-Thon. Is there some cleanup work needed with your internal dialogue? *Pain that has not yet come is avoidable.*

---

27   Ladinsky, p. 48

Supplemental information, support and community for vibers can be found online at www.vibeathon.com.

Remember, what you perceive you receive . . . Now, vibe on!

Day Fourteen: Don't Just Sit There!

Samkalpa implies not only developing our own will but also allying our will with forces that help us achieve its aim.

~ *David Frawley[28]*

John is vibing on manifesting the career of his dreams and is confused about how to distinguish between fantasizing and vibing. Visualizing and vibing on what he wants is one thing, but he is concerned that getting caught up in a daydream can be dangerous, keeping him in a perpetual daze of hope for that someday when he'll magically have what he wants. He's leery of living for tomorrow . . . a mind-set that could become an escapist technique, an excuse for indecision and inertia. He has a few job opportunities right now, but is afraid of making the wrong decision. And he feels like he's trying to talk himself into each opportunity, which is keeping him in a state of confusion and immobility.

Sound familiar? OK, here's the thing. The difference between fantasizing and vibing is that fantasizing is *mental* (using your imagination to start the process of lining up) and vibing is energetic . . . emotional . . . more subtle and experiential. When you begin to fantasize about the job or the love or the money and you get the fantasy up to speed, you begin to feel really good, right? And when you get to that really good-feeling place where you've moved beyond thinking and toward knowing—as though it's just a matter of time before you have what you desire—then you're *vibing*.

When you're vibing, the field of perception opens up to include both evidence of and opportunity for the creation of that which you desire. In John's case, he is looking to manifest the career of his dreams. Currently, opportunities are presenting themselves, but they are not exactly what he's looking for. It's great that he has opened his mind to the extent where those blinders are starting to peel away . . . but this begs the question: Should he act or just keep vibing?

---

28   David Frawley, *Yoga and Ayurveda*, p. 292

I understand the wariness with respect to that potential for escapism and inertia. When we do the work, we begin to see evidence that we are vibing, but it's imperative to remember that nothing will magically appear. No genie in the bottle stuff here—we can't sit and wait and vibe until something perfect appears out of thin air. Evidence will show us that we are on the right path, contrast will show us in what way we are off the path, and as we continue to do the mental work of meditation and mindfulness, the path for creation comes in the form of opportunities. At that point, we take action by exploring the opportunities as they present themselves, while continuing to hone the vibe.

The Bhagavad Gita is a masterpiece about the goals of yoga—absolute peace and abiding in one's true Self. It describes how to attain those objectives through *karma yoga*, the yoga of action. The Gita presents a conversation that takes place on a battlefield as warring relatives prepare to take up arms against each other. In the beginning of the Gita, warrior-prince Arjuna has lost heart and refuses to fight against his kin. Through the course of the story his adviser and charioteer, Lord Krishna, teaches Arjuna how to face the challenges and conflicts of life—how to take action and to win the greatest of battles, that is, how to move away from the externally reaching nature of humanity and toward the internal place where abundance truly lies.

In the third chapter, Lord Krishna instructs:

> *In this world there are two main paths:*
>
> *the yoga of understanding,*
>
> *for contemplative men; and for men*
>
> *who are active, the yoga of action.*
>
> *Not by avoiding actions*
>
> *does a man gain freedom from action,*

and not by renunciation

alone, can he reach the goal.

No one, not even for an instant,

can exist without acting; all beings

are compelled, however unwilling,

by the three strands of Nature called gunas.

He who controls his actions

but lets his mind dwell on sense-objects

is deluding himself and spoiling

his search for the deepest truth.

The superior man is he

whose mind can control his senses;

with no attachment to results,

he engages in the yoga of action.

Do any actions you must do,

since action is better than inaction;

even the existence of your body

depends on necessary actions. (3.3–3.6)[29]

This passage references the gunas, the three elemental qualities of all things in nature. Rajas (simply put, hyperactivity) and tamas (nonactivity) are the qualities that we work to balance, to line ourselves up so that we come to a place of sattva (balance, where vibing takes place).

Coming back to John . . . Say there are five possibilities for work that are catching his interest. He pursues each of them, and in each situation, as he spends time researching the company, interviewing, and learning about the specific job, he pays attention to the details. He sifts through the elements that don't necessarily appeal to him to get to those features that are in sync with what he's looking for. If he finds that one job opportunity matches well, then great! But if John sorts through to get to the good stuff and there isn't so much that's in alignment with the job of his dreams, then that's OK too—because he has discovered evidence that he is getting better at aligning with what he wants and each time, with each opportunity, he will get closer and closer until BOOM! If he truly stays with the vision of what he wants, there will undoubtedly come the day when John realizes that he has manifested the exact situation that he has been looking for.

In this day of unemployment and uncertainty, is it totally ridiculous to think about vibing? Absolutely not! If John finds himself in a situation where he needs to take whatever he can, that's totally OK. The job that he accepts, though it may not be the job of his dreams, will be enough to lessen the stress that comes from not having a job at all. And while he's in this job, he can soothe himself with the knowledge that he has manifested a level of security for himself. If he continues to hold his vision of what he ultimately wants and doesn't get caught up in the details of how it can possibly come to fruition, opportunities will continue to present themselves so that John can move toward where he wants to be.

We can look at any opportunity from one of two standpoints: curiosity or judgment. When we stay in a place of curiosity, the blinders open up a bit more and our widened perception allows us to see a possibility we may never have

---

29 Stephen Mitchell, *Bhagavad Gita*, p. 62

considered. But when we view an opportunity from a stance of judgment, our ego snaps the blinders back into place, keeping us in limited perception. John is a great example of one who chose curiosity, and is well on his way to success because of it.

We never know where the smallest opportunity can lead. In the 1980s, a young singer brought a cassette of his music to a small local deejay, hoping to have it played on air (or at least get some feedback and direction). The deejay wanted to put one of the tracks on a compilation album and, though unenthusiastic about the project, the singer agreed. What the singer failed to recognize at the time was that the small radio station was part of a national chain. He (Jon Bon Jovi) received national recognition, formed a band. And that, my friends, is not only rock and roll history—it's a great example of how to create by maintaining an easy, curious attitude about taking opportunities.

There are thousands of examples of what can happen when we take an opportunity, even if it doesn't seem like a perfect fit.

All things are possible, but we're here to create and be and *do things* . . . not to sit and create by magic. We use the fantasy to get to the vibration . . . we use the vibration to draw to us the experiences and opportunities that we're looking to create . . . and then we create them. So get out there and create!

In the field of opportunity, it's plowing time again

~ Neil Young, "Field of Opportunity"

For Today:

1. Continue with meditation.

2. For consideration: In your daily life, are you beginning to see evidence showing you that you are on the right path toward what you want? How about opportunities? Remember, the opportunities may not be exactly what you specifically want, but may be the stepping-stone you need to get you on the path to what you do want. So take a shot!

Supplemental information, support and community for vibers can be found online at www.vibeathon.com.

Remember, what you perceive you receive . . . Now, vibe on!

Week Three

Let's start with a vibration story to get us into the swing of things for the week, shall we?

Many moons ago, I found a cool brown bag in a catalog . . . and immediately fell in love. Didn't care how much it cost, didn't care whether I needed it or not—as Romeo recognized when he first glanced at Juliet, I knew it was to be mine. I called the store and placed my order. The salesperson on the phone assured me it was on the way.

I happily carried on with my life.

At this time, I was working in the corporate world. A few weeks had passed since I placed the order, and my assistant asked if I had received the bag yet. I hadn't thought that much about it because the salesperson told me it was on the way, but since I hadn't yet received it, I called the store to inquire. I spoke with a different salesperson, who informed me that she didn't know who I had previously spoken with, but the bag was on back order until at least the year 2050 and she was sorry for the delay but there was nothing she could do.

For the briefest of moments, I felt again as Romeo—now having come upon the seemingly lifeless body of his beloved. Then, as quickly, I remembered that I was learning to vibe in other areas of my life, and figured this would be as good a time as any to put it to use. I put down the phone and immediately commenced vibing on getting the bag that very same day. When doubts came up I did the mental work to come back into alignment, closer to the place on the vibrational spectrum of having the bag on my shoulder in the next few hours. Again, I went on with my day.

As I was leaving the office, the bag had not arrived. I kept mining my thoughts away from doubt and futility and holding my vision.

At that time, I was juggling work with teaching yoga and left the office in mid-town Manhattan for the Upper East Side to teach a class. I took the subway up to 77th Street and made my way to 3rd Avenue. As I walked down the street, I glanced up at one of the stores along the way. On a mannequin in a window was . . . MY BAG! I had successfully opened my mind up to the possibility of getting the bag without getting caught up in the details of how it would happen, and in doing so my field of perception opened up to include finding it in a small shop on 3rd Avenue. I went into the store and asked the salesperson to take it down, and on close inspection I confirmed that, indeed, it was the exact bag I was waiting for . . . the same one that I was vibing on.

As if that wasn't wonderful enough, the salesperson informed me that everything in the store was 20 percent off. So, not only did I get my bag as I had vibed, but I purchased it for less money than anticipated.

I've thought about the lesson of that bag often. Why did it happen so smoothly? Why did it seem as though all I had to do was hold a simple thought et voilà— whereas a million other things that I'd tried to create seemed so long and hard to come to?

The answer may be that there was not so much emotional attachment to the bag. Don't get me wrong . . . I really wanted it! But it wasn't to the same degree as the big things in life that we work to manifest—the love, the career, the various forms of security, and the peace.

It was easy for me to manifest the bag because there wasn't any baggage attached to it (pun intended). I lined up and then was able to let go. And in letting go, what I was really doing was letting go of the ego constraints that want to control everything and that do so from the confines of previous conditioning and experience.

The bag was a small thing. But with the "big" things, it's not always so easy to line up vibrationally, especially if what you're currently experiencing—and what you've learned to expect from the past experience and conditioning we know as *samskaras*—seems very far from what you want to be or do or have.

You've been vibing on the subject of your Vibe-a-Thon for the past two weeks. As you think about that which you are working toward, where are you? Are you in a place of hopeful, positive expectation? Or are you still arguing for your limitations? People often say "I want things to be different than they are . . . I need things to be different than they are." And they spend so much time focusing on the fact that they want things to be different than they are *instead of how they want things to be* that their vibration stays focused on things *as they are*.

But the fact is, things are as they are in the present moment. And we have to accept the present moment—to make the best of things as they are—in order to ever get anywhere.

One of the most important things to learn on this vibrational path is to be here and clear, present and content in the moment. The present moment is the vantage point that shows us exactly where we are on the vibrational spectrum. It's the place where we can accurately perceive the thoughts and emotions that are helping or holding us back from creating. The clearer we are in our minds, the more open to possibilities we feel. The better we feel, the stronger the alignment. And when there is alignment, we are well on our way.

How do we do that? It's not a difficult thing in theory:

- Talk about *what you perceive* as your current state of reality less and talk about what you're *creating* more.

- Talk about things that are bothering you less and talk about things that make you feel good more.

- Talk about things that are going wrong less and talk about things that are going right more.

For example, imagine that we're in a workshop together. It is a once-in-a-lifetime gathering where we will learn about a subject that is riveting to each and every participant in individual ways, and we can't wait to get started.

One hour into the workshop, construction workers directly outside the building begin using jackhammers and drills, creating distraction and frustration. Just an hour earlier, the conditions were much more conducive to digesting this wonderful, fascinating material. What would you do? Remember, this is the workshop you've been waiting for your entire life . . . and it's never going to be offered again! Would you leave? No, you want to understand this new information.

What we have (noise) is what we have, so we have to shift the focus. We have to come to the practice of *dharana*—bringing our attention back to our point of focus and away from the noise, whether represented by jackhammers or the disallowing thoughts that keep us from opening to new possibilities and paths. In this way, we actively shape our perception to include what we want, and block out what we don't want.

Lamenting the fact that it was better before the jackhammers started up only causes a vibration that disallows what we want (to immerse ourselves in the workshop), because the focus is on the noise. But we *can* get back, set our attention so much on what we want from the workshop that we would be oblivious to anything that is happening outside.

When I was young, my mom had the uncanny ability to direct her focus toward what she wanted when having a phone conversation with one of her friends (a break that she so deserved, with six children and rarely a moment to herself). One of my younger brothers would try to get her attention, either by poking her arm incessantly or taking hold of her chin and trying to turn her face toward him. She would calmly disengage her son, kiss him on top of the head, and continue her conversation. A brilliant example of keeping the focus where you want it to be.

This is what we need to do anytime we encounter thoughts that are not really along the track of what we'd like to experience. We need to play down the part of it that is not in vibrational alignment with what we want by beating the rhythm of what we do want to the extent that it becomes our pervasive state of being—so much so that it becomes the new perception. Because *what you perceive you receive.*

When we get rolling, vibing on what we want, the distractions become less important. As the alignment with our thoughts builds momentum, what seemed a nuisance before (i.e., jackhammers) seems unimportant now because there is so much connection *inside* with what we want. And it's exactly the same with what you're working to manifest. You need to get so aligned with what you want that you drown out any reverberation or vibration that has to do with whatever it is that you do not want. You harness your attention on what you want, tune out everything else, and make great strides on the path of creating.

And what of those who have not yet learned alignment and focus? Well, they will leave the workshop feeling nothing but frustration and hearing jackhammers in their heads. Because that's what they focused on.

But wait! There's more! Besides the fact that you focused on what you wanted, you also began to understand that the noise outside the workshop—or those big, bad, discordant thoughts—were a blessing in disguise. Why? *Because it showed you the contrast of what you didn't want so that you could focus your attention on what you did want.* In effect, we become thankful for the noise outside the workshop because it reminds us of who we are and what we want to create—and showcases our infinite ability to do so.

It's essential to understand that the present moment is OK, because it becomes the platform from which we rework, refocus, and realign. And by learning to stop condemning the present moment, we can learn to relax into it. From that place of calm, we can continue to soothe ourselves toward what we want by observing the contrast that will allow continued refinement of the vibration.

The first sutra, *Atha yoganusasanam* is broadly translated as "yoga is now." When the mind, body, and spirit are yoked together as one and when we are fully present in the moment, we are in the exploration of yoga. We accomplish this unwavering presence by calming the mind so that it rests in a place of peace, thereby coming to a place of Oneness with our Soul, our true Self, the God within—you get the picture. At all other times, we identify with our thoughts. In the example that we have been exploring, when we identify with the noise of the jackhammers it takes us away from our point of focus.

The less we identify with the thoughts and impressions outside of us (i.e., the noise), the more we are at one with ourselves. From there we can accurately choose the thoughts that are in line with what we wish to create, thereby moving onto the path toward manifestation.

Your reality is perceived. And your perception is a compilation of thoughts. Once you realize that thoughts shape your perception, you realize that by changing the thoughts you can soothe yourself toward the perception—and manifestation—that you seek. And when you've discovered that you can soothe yourself, you've got the key to everything, because soothing yourself brings you to a place of *allowing*. And every time you change the way you feel the slightest little bit, that slight soothing shifts you vibrationally to a whole new path.

It doesn't take much shift in the frequency to tap into something entirely different than what you've been attracting. Sometimes, turning a radio dial by the slightest bit will bring in an entirely new set of music or a whole new set of discussions. The only difference here is that the dial is our mind, and by clearing up our thoughts we open our field of perception and shift our vibrational frequency to include the things we want.

It's really worth making the effort to soothe yourself, because as you do, your vibration shifts to something a little better . . . and a little better. And the better you feel, the easier it becomes to focus your thoughts and harness your vision. Not only because your perception is shifting to allow you to experience the better-feeling stuff, but because you also gain the confidence with every shift that it's going to be all right and that you can make yourself feel OK under any and all conditions.

A few weeks after my fantastic bag incident, I experienced another opportunity to show myself how well vibing can work. I was a marketing associate at a private equity firm, working on press releases and other time-sensitive issues. It was one of the days I needed to leave the office at a decent hour to teach my 6:00 p.m. yoga class. Five o'clock came and went, and as I prepared to leave the office a senior partner appeared at my door, talking a mile a minute. They were on the brink of closing a major, gazillion-dollar deal and I was expected in his office in five minutes to figure out the press strategy, which he wanted on the wires that evening. Of course, I was needed to spearhead the entire thing.

I immediately froze up. If I didn't leave the office in fifteen minutes, I wouldn't make it to teach the class. And what I wanted was to teach the class. My stomach turned and my nerves began a mad rumba of anxiety.

Then I remembered the lesson I had taught myself with the bag.

I told the partner I would be in his office for the meeting . . . and I got down to my real work.

I closed my door and kicked off my shoes. I got down on the ground directly behind the door and threw my legs up the wall. I closed my eyes and spent the next five minutes inhaling and exhaling . . . and setting my vibe on how I wanted the meeting to go. I started a mantra in my mind, "He's going to tell me that we can't do a release tonight . . . He's going to tell me that we can't do a release tonight . . . I will get out of here on time . . ."

I went into his office, holding the thoughts and keeping myself as calm as possible . . . all the while, remembering the lesson of my previous vibrational success. I sat down with the others and began to take notes as he spewed his plans for this very important release to those in the room.

I held the thought . . . took notes . . . repeated my mantra . . . answered questions . . . held the thought. And then, in midstream he said:

"Wait . . . I forgot . . . We can't do the release tonight."

He had remembered there were legal implications to the deal that required silence. Did lining up my thoughts about leaving on time shift not only my perspective, but his as well? On day six we looked at some photos by Dr. Masaru Emoto and saw the effects that thoughts had on the crystallization of water molecules. The 1993 research of Jacobo Grinberg-Zylberbaum was offered as evidence of the capacity for our thoughts to effect change in another human's brain activity—demonstrating the ability of two people, meditating together with the intention of direct communication, to share the effects of stimulation to one brain.

Perhaps my surety in making it to class superseded his desire to put out the release. Or maybe it was the combined mutual desire of all the others in the room who wanted to finish the day and make their way home. And, no, it's not magic—although it is pretty cool when you see that it works so well . . . not to mention how practical it can be!

In the moment when the partner spoke to me in my office, my state of being was not in line with creating what I wanted. Previous conditioning and experience had wrapped around me in a heavy blanket of thoughts such as *I can't get out of this*, and *I'm going to get in trouble*, leading up to the ever-popular *It's impossible for me to have what I want*. And in the period of time that I had, I knew I wasn't easily going to be able to talk myself into a better-feeling place. So I reached into my Vibrational Emergency Management Kit (VEMK), the vast array of things that I know help calm me down on a physical level, which soothes my energy and allows me to get back on a path to realignment.

There are times when we feel so out of sync with what we want that it seems almost impossible to get ourselves back on track. But even at those times there are things that can help you feel better. And once you utilize one or two or twenty of the things that are available to each and every one of us— soothing yourself on the physical plane so that the nerves calm—you'll see that in any situation, you can bring yourself slowly back into alignment. And at times you may feel so out of whack that it takes a longer period of time than you would like, but that's OK. What you are looking to create is not going anywhere.

The moments when we find we need to soothe ourselves are often the result of stress. Stress is a reaction to a stimulus, a response that triggers the production of hormones and their release throughout the body, sending alarm signals to the vital systems necessary to get us out of danger. Stress in dangerous situations is a good thing because it keeps us safe. Psychological stress—as happens when we react to challenging situations— creates the same hormonal response. And so the more we can understand the things that trigger a stress reaction within, the more we can find and use tools to deactivate the response as it plays out through the body.

We can also explore this through the gunas. The gunas are sometimes described as energies, sometimes as qualities, though no English word can define their whole nature and function. Collectively, they may be thought of as a triangle of forces, opposed yet complementary. They exist to serve us, to provide information about our state in the present moment so that we can effect change that brings us back to status quo. Rajas is frenetic, agitated energy. When rajas dominates, it is almost as though we are caffeinated. When we are in a rajasic state of mind, thoughts are darting and focus is quite out of the question. Tamas is the opposite, seen as heavy, dull, and lethargic. When in a tamasic state, the mind acts like it is stuck in mud. Sattva is clarity, luminosity, and serenity. It is the state that we are working toward through the practices of mindfulness and meditation. When in a rajasic state we can incorporate some qualities of tamas to bring us to sattva, and vice versa. Balance is available to us on every level, at every moment.

Isn't it great to know that, in fact, you truly do have full control over your well-being? You are the driver of the car. The car is your body and the chatter of the mind is the sound of the radio within the car, but you are the driver. Full control!

The tools that we all utilize to make us feel better are as unique and individualized as we are. So I'll share with you some of the tried and true things I use when I know my vibration needs some real supercharging. These are part of my own VEMK, but feel free to use them as a starting point in creating your own tools.

MUSIC

I would have to say that this is my number one go-to item when I'm feeling off my path. I can be completely out of whack, but if I take some time and listen to music that makes me feel good, I feel so much better. And the thing I felt so out of whack with? After some music, somehow it doesn't seem so bad. Music is vibrational, and it recharges in such a great way.

I have a playlist named "SHIFT!!!" The list contains many songs—everything from the "Hallelujah Chorus" to Led Zeppelin's "Immigration Song," from some great songs from my childhood to songs that I recorded with my band years ago. If anyone ever spent time going through this list, I'm sure they would think I'm crazy. But each and every one of the songs reminds me of something good or powerful or free—all the things that make me feel great and line me up vibrationally. Create a playlist, or burn a CD of different UPBEAT songs that you love.

COLLECTING EVIDENCE

If you're feeling way off the path of what you want, look around and begin to collect evidence of your desire's growing manifestation in your life. For example, if you are trying to realign with your desire for more money, begin to collect evidence of money in your life. Make a list of every time you've paid a bill; or look at a penny on the street as evidence of your own abundance and security; watch a movie or read a book about someone who made a great deal of money against all the odds; even find evidence in the plethora of lotteries out there and available to you. Whatever you can find that will soothe you and help you to feel better, collect evidence of it!

EXERCISE

Get your yah-yahs out! Take a yoga class; go for a walk or a run outside; put on some music and jump around your living room . . . anything that will get your energy moving is going to help you to soothe yourself, and relieve some of the effects of stress on your body. Further, exercise boosts brainpower. When we exercise, the brain produces BDNF, a protein that amplifies neurotransmitter responses and promotes synaptic connection[30]. BDNF is basically like Miracle-Gro for the brain.

TAKE A SHOWER

As you let the water cascade down over you, imagine the troubled thoughts or negative emotions pouring down the drain with the water. Stay as long as you need to allow the negativity to "wash off." When you get out of the shower, use some essential oils to bring yourself further back into alignment.

GET BACK TO NAURE

Take a walk, look at the trees, watch the water in a pond, or dig in the dirt with your toes and/or fingers. Nature is the universe's most pure manifestation. Reconnecting with it can allow for an amazing reconnection with the Self.

KIDS AND PETS

I come from a large family, and my nieces and nephews bring me great joy. When I spend time with them, I get down to their level. I play with them. I color with them. I talk to them and listen to the magical way they think about things. And the more I stay at their level, the more things at "my level" begin to make sense. It's the same thing with animals. I can be completely in a funk, and yet if I take some time to watch and play with my cat or go to Central Park and watch the dogs walking, running, and playing, I feel completely soothed and relaxed.

---

30   Boesman et al, 2007 (http://gut.bmj.com/content/57/3/314.abstract)

CREATE THE MOVIE VERSION OF YOU

This is a great technique. Imagine yourself as the subject of a movie, in the middle of the bad-feeling dilemma you are currently experiencing. Can you turn it into a comedy? No need to actually write yourself out of it, but spend some time in the experience of how the protagonist (you!) turns the tables and finds a way to get exactly what he or she desires. And have fun with it!

INDUCE THE RELAXATION RESPONSE

Coined by Dr. Herbert Benson in 1975, the term *relaxation response* describes the elicitation of the parasympathetic nervous system to lessen the effects of stress on the body and mind. Any repetitive action can be used to induce the effect, from jogging or walking to knitting, golfing, gardening, cleaning, or any other activity that you find relaxing. In order to gain the benefits of the parasympathetic mode through the relaxation response, you must bring two components into play:

1. Engage in a repetitive activity;

2. Set the intention to relax while performing the activity.

There is no success or failure with this technique! As long as you set the intention to relax, you have begun to elicit the benefits of the relaxation response.

SLEEP

Sometimes the best thing we can do is to recognize that the negative mood is with us for the day—and to set the intention to get a good night's sleep and begin fresh in the morning.

TAKE A BREAK!

If you feel that you are trying so hard to hold your vibration that it feels more like a death grip than anything else, take a break from it. Keep your mind on other things that feel good, with the knowledge that your desired manifestation is not going anywhere. And remember—you can be or do or have anything you want . . . but you don't have to be or do or have it all right this minute! If it's more stressful than anything to think about it, then don't.

Always remember that you have full control over your own well-being. And you can feel contentment in any given moment because you know that all reality is perceived. You know that, by doing the work of mindfulness and meditation, thoughts come into alignment with what you are looking to create, and that feels good. The better you feel, the easier it is to line up vibrationally . . . and with your Vibrational Emergency Management Kit, you have the tools to always find a way to feel OK. My word, you're getting more powerful by the minute!

Exercises for Week Three

Exercise #1: Create your personal VEMK (Vibrational Emergency Management Kit)

1. Come up with five or six different things that you feel will help you get synced up if/when you're out of whack. Try to make each thing unique and distinct from the others, so that you have a wide range of options available to you when you're reaching for a better-feeling place.

2. Once you have this list, take out the sheet of paper you created in the first week of the Vibe-a-Thon (describing your life with successful attainment of your desire). Write VEMK in an empty part of the page and write your list of go-to items underneath.

3. Use each of the tools at least once over the course of the next week. Make a mental note of how each of the tools helps you emotionally or vibrationally, as well as a promise to yourself to USE THE TOOLS as necessary.

Exercise #2: Collect Evidence

1. Make a list of the times in your life when you have wanted something and it came effortlessly, almost magically to you. What was the experience like? Did you have to focus your attention on those things, or was it a more playful, hopeful, easy focus?

2. Begin to create a list of the evidence that you are lining up more and more. Remember, this list doesn't have to be about only the big things: if you're working to manifest love and you see someone who represents some of the characteristics you're looking for, take it as evidence.

Meditation: The Session

1. 5 minutes—Alternate Nostril Breathing (i.e., *Nadi Shodhana*)

2. 5 minutes—Breath Awareness

3. 10–15 minutes—Effortful Concentration (*Dharana*)

4. 5–7 minutes—Visualization

Supplemental information, support and community for vibers can be found online at www.vibeathon.com.

Remember, what you perceive you receive . . . Now, vibe on to week three!

Day Sixteen: Now . . . Let Go!

Seek refuge in the attitude of detachment and you will amass the wealth of spiritual awareness. The man who is motivated only by desire for the fruits of his actions and anxious about the results is miserable indeed. (The Bhagavad Gita 2.49)[31]

One of the most challenging things to learn is how to let go in order to allow the evidence and opportunities to present. We desire something and do our work to change the perception. Without realizing it, in holding and holding and holding our vision, we can begin to create anxiety about the when and how of the results. Anxiety comes from the ego, which is both trying with all its might to control the limits of the current field of perception (because that is what it knows and relies on to feed itself) and sending warning signals out to the entire body that somebody is trying to shake things up.

Somebody *is* trying to shake things up. It's YOU! So you fight you. And then what do we get? More anxiety, less ability to open the mind—so, fewer results.

The subject of your Vibe-a-Thon is like a seed that has been planted. It was well planted in good soil, watered, and provided with plenty of suitable sunlight so it can grow into the perfect version of whatever type of plant it is meant to be. Is it necessary to dig up the little seedling every few moments to see if it has grown? We all know that such an action would crush any chance of that poor seed actually manifesting.

More likely, you would plant the seed and then let it grow. Water it as necessary, replant only if the sun is not finding it readily. Other than attending to it appropriately, you would hang back and watch as it came into fruition.

Can you do that a bit more with the subject of your Vibe-a-Thon?

---

31   Eknath Easwaran, *The Bhagavad Gita*, p. 89

As mentioned, the philosophy of yoga is concerned with the attainment of peace of mind, with stilling the thoughts so that we come to a place of Oneness with All That Is. Calming the thoughts is a vital component in being able to discern and create thoughts that are in line with what we are choosing to manifest in our lives, and the ideas of practice (*abhyasa*) and letting go or nonattachment (*vairagya*) are important concepts to review.

Practice and all is coming.

~ Pattabhi Jois

In vibing, we practice by attending to our vision, making sure that we are staying lined up vibrationally with what we want. We know that sutra 1.13 identifies the qualities that define practice as consistency over a long period of time and with passion or interest. This is really very logical, isn't it? The amount of time it takes to truly change our perception about something (and therefore, our reality) will depend on the consistency just mentioned as well as on the depth of adverse *samskaras* (deeply held patterns of disallowing thoughts) associated with what you are looking to create. The less divergent our thoughts, the easier it is to stay lined up. Lastly—and again, just as obvious—we have to stay interested. This is relatively simple when we are in the beginning stages of vibing, where the excitement can be akin to having our name called to "Come on down!" as the next contestant on the Game Show of Life.

That passion and interest is just as necessary on those days when the emerging evidence isn't so easy to identify.

There is a practice of practice! If we are attending to our vibe every once in a while, it will take longer for it to become manifest than if we are attending to it regularly. Makes sense, doesn't it? If we only water our little plant once every month, it's not going to do as well as if we water it every day or so.

Nonattachment, with respect to vibing, means not getting caught up in the details—knowing that you have done your work to line up and then staying content in the moment, understanding that it's just a matter of time before what you desire is fully created. The Sanskrit word for nonattachment is *vairagya*, meaning "without color." It surfaces when the mind voluntarily switches its intrinsic motivations away from the identifications of the ego—which we experience as our current perception of reality—and into the field of infinite possibility.

Human beings are control freaks! In the case of the subject of your Vibe-a-Thon, it may be the anxiety of the why or how or *if* that keeps you in a place of trying to figure out how to figure it out. Nonattachment brings fearlessness in that you are no longer concerned about the if, when, and how. It opens us up to allow manifestation. In the same way that sitting against a door will keep the door from opening, in nonattachment we move away from the door and it is free to open wide. Have you ever searched for something only to find that the second you stop looking it appears? That's nonattachment.

In nonattachment, we move into a state of expansion as we quite literally widen our field of perception. If we are doing the work of being present and mindful about what's happening, expansion will feel like mild excitement mixed with just a hint of tentativeness – because we are moving into the unknown. It's akin to the feeling of climbing to the top of the first hill of a roller coaster. If we don't interpret that sense of expansion correctly it can feel strangely similar to anxiety, often causing reversion to old patterns of reactive behavior. And closing off new possibilities.

Here's the thing: If you already had the subject of your Vibe-a-Thon in your life, you wouldn't be in a place of trying to vibe on it, right? Soooo, the blinders currently surrounding your field of perception haven't opened yet to reveal the new opportunities and evidence that will get you to where you want to go. And the only way to open your field of perception to include those prospects is to let go so that those blinders can peel away. It isn't what you desire that is causing grief. It's the mental death grip that you are holding it in!

A baby seagull will peer out over the side of its nest, fearful of the fall below. When its mother nudges the bird out of the nest, it will flap its wings reactively, hoping upon hope to figure out what needs to be done. As young seagulls grow and learn, it's an amazing thing to watch them, one after the other, as they give up control over their own bodies and allow the wind to hold them and carry them onward. As though giving in, living in the moment, allows them to go much farther than if they tried to control their bodies and make the movement happen by force.

Stay focused on what you want, but let go of the need to control the how and when and where. As B. K. S. Iyengar said, practice and letting go are like the two wings of a bird. Without one, the bird cannot fly.

For Today:

1. Continue with meditation.

2. For consideration: Focus on your exhale—exhaling is symbolic of letting go, and quite often our inhaling is significantly deeper than our exhaling. From a physiological perspective, this means that we basically inhale on top of inhale and nearly hyperventilate ourselves. In exhaling, we create the space for the next inhale to come in. And in letting go, we allow what's coming. So, take a few moments today, notice the exhale, and let it go—

Supplemental information, support and community for vibers can be found online at www.vibeathon.com.

Remember, what you perceive you receive ... Now, vibe on!

Day Seventeen: The Next Logical Step

Hopefully, as you have been vibing and as your field of perception has started to widen, evidence indicating that the subject of your Vibe-a-Thon is beginning to come into fruition has been unveiled. This can take any form—for example, if you are working to manifest more financial security and have been harnessing your vibe toward having more money, perhaps you have come across a five-dollar bill you had forgotten about in the pocket of a jacket. Evidence can be small or large, and the more we notice all of the bits suggesting that we are on the right path, the better. No matter how small or unimpressive it may seem, evidence is evidence. And your open-minded ability to accept it as evidence will facilitate the further opening of your mind.

When we are vibing, we rarely go from *not having* to *having* in a heartbeat. For the most part it happens gradually, in the same way that your vibration has been lining up . . . gradually. The process of changing the way we think about something—altering those underlying thought patterns we know as *samskaras*—happens when we are consistent in the practice, over a long period of time, and with passion.

In driving from one side of whatever continent you're on to the other, the closer you get to your destination the more signs you see that point to where you're going. If driving from New York to California, would you expect to see signs for the destination in Ohio? Of course not. But the closer you get to California, the more evidence you will see that the destination is just a little further along the way. So you stay the course, until your ultimate goal becomes the next logical step.

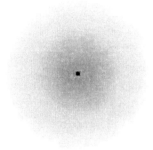

Take a look at this optical illusion. Keep your focus on the dot until the gray matter around it disappears. In those first few moments of concentration, the eyes
naturally dart back and forth from the dot to the entire image, in the same way
that those persistent disallowing beliefs will sneak in when we start the process of
vibing and take us away from the understanding that anything is possible.

There comes a moment when you've almost come to one-pointed focus
with the black dot. Just . . . right . . . there! At that instant you could let
go of the focus on the point and shift your perception back to the entire
image—yet if you choose to keep your focus on the point, the rest of the
gray matter surrounding the dot will in fact appear to disappear. You will
no longer perceive it.

Do you recognize that your work is to stay in an open, nonreactive state of mind
in your daily life so that you can sift through the disallowing thought patterns and
fine-tune your vibe? And that by consciously choosing to hold your vision in those
moments of distraction, you'll be closer to perceiving the next logical step?

As we know, meditation is the training ground for the mind, where we soften
the chatter in the brain's left hemisphere and open to the possibilities "outside
the box" in the right hemisphere. As we do the work of stilling, focusing, and
thus opening the mind within our practice, those tools become more readily

available for us in daily life, and the detail-oriented left brain is reconditioned through our mindfulness to look for evidence in line with our vibe.

In his authoritative work *The Heart of Yoga*, T. K. V. Desikachar describes *vinyasa krama* as a step-by-step approach or a thoughtful process. "*Krama* is the step, *nyasa* means 'to place,' and the prefix *vi-* translates as 'in a special way.' "[32] In learning to do anything, there are dues to be paid. To become proficient in playing an instrument, there are notes, chords, and simple patterns to be conquered before taking on any masterful work. And after you've done the grunt work for what may appear to be a long period of time, your ability to play music changes: at first you could play just a series of chords or a few notes; now you can play something more intrinsically musical. This illustrates what we have all experienced at moments in our lives, when we suddenly "get" something that has required us to shift into a new context of thinking: making sense of a mathematical concept we initially struggled with, figuring out a puzzle, or getting the symbolic meaning that underlies a story. As in learning, when we do the work of honing our vibe through creating the space in meditation and staying diligently mindful in our daily life, at some point the work will lead us directly toward that which we desire.

As you play with vibing in your day-to-day existence, you begin to see evidence of and opportunity for the manifestation of that which you desire. This builds up confidence in your ability to create, and you begin to understand that manifestation is not a big "WOW" thing, because when you get your vibration truly lined up with the vision you're working to manifest, you are in such a state of Oneness and belief and *knowing* that manifestation is simply the next logical step.

When what we want feels very far away from possible, we're not lined up. And the more lined up we are, the more possible it seems. It may be that you are 99.99 percent lined up before the evidence and opportunities start pouring in because some part of you is still in a disallowing state. Remember, those deeply held negative patterns can really be DEEP. But as you continue to do your work, eventually you will get to the place where you are more in belief that your desire will become manifest than you are in disbelief. Then your certainty is unwavering and manifestation is the next logical step.

---

32   T. K. V. Desikachar, *The Heart of Yoga*, p. 25

Isn't that logical?

For Today:

1. Continue with meditation.

2. For consideration: Collect evidence. As you make your way through the day, continually collect evidence that supports what you are working to create. Remember, nothing is too small or inconsequential! If you find that you are coming up against contrast, make a concerted effort to identify exactly what the contrasting evidence is there to show you. Everything is there to help you line up with what you want . . . there is no good or bad.

Supplemental information, support and community for vibers can be found online at www.vibeathon.com.

Remember, what you perceive you receive . . . Now, vibe on!

Day Eighteen: Is This All Too Good to Be True?

NO!

That's the simple answer and the absolute truth. But it does beg a question: Are you willing to believe that you can actually have what you want?

Most of us have beliefs that can make it challenging to fully line up and create. A viber can try his or her best to create a vision, line up with it and hold on, but if there is a disallowing belief lurking around in the background it's like snuffing out a birthday candle before you make a wish and blow it out.

A belief is a *samskara*—simply a thought you think over and over again. In the same way that lifting heavy boxes repeatedly without bending the knees will cause a repetitive stress injury to the lower back, *samskaras* will create certain patterns. And when those beliefs become deeply ingrained as part of our personality, they turn into major obstacles or *klesas*. The *klesas*—ignorance, egoism, desire, aversion, and fear—cloud over the truer part of ourselves, the part that knows all things are possible without limit or boundary.

We have conscious and subconscious parts of the mind. The conscious mind is filled up with the chatter and thoughts that run actively (and sometimes haphazardly), filling our waking attention. The conscious mind is also where we do the work of creating thoughts and new *samskaras* that are in line with the desire we are trying to fulfill. The subconscious part of the mind is the warehouse, storing all of our previous experiences and conditioning that culminate in habitual, reactive patterns of response.

The conscious and subconscious parts of the mind are not separate but rather fully interdependent, and yet the subconscious mind is *more* powerful because those reactive patterns have been hiding out at the gym, doing push-ups and getting stronger each and every time they have been activated. "When it comes to sheer neurological processing abilities, the subconscious mind is millions of times more powerful than the conscious mind. If the desires of the conscious mind conflict with the programs in the subconscious mind, which mind do you think will win out?"[33]

We all have experiences that push our buttons and potentially cause us to fly off the handle. In understanding that they are the simple stimulus-response of a behavior pattern stored in the subconscious mind, we can begin to do the work of getting to the seed of that reaction in order to deactivate it.

In 1985, Hurricane Gloria hit the East Coast. I had graduated college a few months earlier and was commuting from my home in New Jersey to my first job in the Big Apple. Every morning, Pops and I would drive to Westwood where he would take the train and I would hop on the bus to Port Authority, and although the weather reports predicted what was to come, that morning my father and I decided to head in.

By the time the bus came out of the Lincoln Tunnel to the terminal, a full-on storm was raging. And yet (call it stupidity of youth, I don't know) I decided to walk to my building instead of taking the subway. There I was, sheets and sheets of rain battering me and wind almost knocking me off balance. When I reached Times Square, I realized what a ridiculous choice it had been to walk the distance, as there was nobody else in the vicinity. Except for one man. And this poor man was clutching onto his umbrella for dear life, even though the fabric from it was completely gone. There was absolutely no possibility that its skeleton could serve him in any way . . . In fact, one could argue that the metal could have conducted electricity if there was a lightening strike.

Is what you're holding onto—mentally or otherwise—serving you? We've spent a good deal of time now on clearing the space through meditation, and mindfully cultivating those conscious thoughts that are in line with what we are looking to create. But unless we go deeper into the recesses of our subconscious mind and do our best to clear the reactive thoughts in *that* realm, we will continue to experience limitation and boundaries regardless of how good our conscious vibe is.

There is a process to identify when the deeper impressions are influencing our ability to vibe. Are you able to visualize and think in line with what you want

---

33   Bruce Lipton, *The Biology of Belief*, p. 97

for the most part, yet deep inside there is a sneaking suspicion that you're kidding yourself? Are you swimming in a sea of contrast? Do opportunities present themselves that will take you even the teeniest step closer to creating and yet somehow you either never take that step or subtly sabotage yourself?

In the same way that a weed needs to be dug up by the root in order to remove it completely, we need to do the work of finding the root of the reactive patterns that no longer serve us. We identify the root of the weed by following it down from flower to stem to root, and we can trace our *samskaras* back to their root by contemplating earlier, similar thoughts. When you think about what it is you are trying to manifest, what kind of negative thoughts come up? Try to identify one negative thought (or area where you are concerned about your ability to manifest that particular thing—i.e., "I can't because . . ."). From there, backtrack. That deeply held belief didn't just pop out of nowhere! Though it may take a bit of time and digging, try (from that first disallowing thought) to come to an earlier, similar thought—a memory of a previous time when similar feelings occurred. It's a fascinating process and you may be quite surprised at where you wind up.

Once you have arrived at the earliest similar thought, deactivate it! It's all in your head anyway, and even if it is based on an actual experience, remember that the experience is over. Soften it in your mind and soothe the emotions attached to it so that it no longer keeps you from the good things you so richly deserve. Because yes, it really is all good and getting better if you believe it is. And it's NOT too good to be true.

There is an ancient Indian story about a sculptor who was so gifted that his statues almost seemed to come to life out of the stone. Once, lost in admiration over his stone elephants, one of his students asked, "How do you do this? These elephants are more real than real elephants are; you can almost hear them trumpeting." And the sculptor replied, "There's no secret to it. I just go and get a big block of stone, set it up in my studio, and study it very carefully. Then I take my hammers and chisels and slowly, over a number of years, I chip away everything that is not elephant."

Happy chipping!

For Today:

1.   Continue with meditation.

2.   For consideration: Trace your earlier similar thoughts—

   a.   Try to identify one negative thought (or area where you are
        concerned about your ability to manifest a particular thing).
        Remember, this may very well present itself as a feeling state
        as well as a thought. If it's a feeling that comes up, try to look
        deeper into it to get at the thought that caused the feeling
        state.

   b.   Identify an earlier, similar thought. When, before your current
        experience of that thought, did you experience it?

   c.   Continue backtracking (what's the precursor to the earlier,
        similar thought?) until you hit on something that is either
        significant or as far back as you can go. Don't be surprised if it
        goes way back to childhood.

   d.   Deactivate it! Soften it in your mind and soothe the emotions
        attached to it so that it no longer keeps you from the good
        things you are looking to create.

Supplemental information, support and community for vibers can be found
online at www.vibeathon.com.

Remember, what you perceive you receive . . . Now, vibe on!

Day Nineteen: Mind Your Own Business!

You can't buy into someone else's trip.

~ Ram Dass

The only thing that has anything to do with you is *where you are in relationship to where you want to be.*

Where are you on your vibrational spectrum? Holding the vision, making the adjustments necessary by integrating evidence, discerning contrast, and taking the opportunities that are unveiled to move you further toward what you are trying to create . . . or are you beginning to look around at *everyone else's* progress (or lack thereof) as they make their way on their path? Where they are is where they are, and it has absolutely nothing to do with you, your desires, and your vibrational alignment with those desires.

It's time to stop measuring where you are in relationship to where anybody else is. Wherever you are is just fine. Your desires are fine; where you currently stand in relation to those desires is fine; and where everyone else is on their path is fine as well.

When we look to the experience of others, we are actually taking ourselves out of sync with our own vibe and into the exploration of their experience. I witness this frequently when teaching a challenging pose such as an arm balance to a group of students. They pay close attention as I demonstrate how to coordinate body parts and move safely into the pose—and when it is time for them to give it a shot, I see two approaches:

- Students who keep their attention focused on what's going on with their own body on their own mat will generally come into some approximation of the shape. They may not come fully into the balance, but there is control and focus.

- Students who start by focusing on what's going on with their own body on their own mat, but as soon as they question their strength or ability they look around at everyone else. These students either fall flat on their faces or never get beyond the beginning stages of the pose.

This is much the same circumstance as when we take the focus off ourselves and place it misguidedly onto someone else.

Human beings are evolutionarily engineered with a negativity bias. Because of this we either consciously or unconsciously look at others as potential threats to our own security. If we are looking at the experience of others from a place of insecurity or doubt about our own power to create, our perception of their experience will manifest as subtle or not so subtle feelings that something is missing or lacking in us. Moreover, because of the competitive nature of the ego and the desire to survive and *win*, we become irresistibly interested in inspecting and scrutinizing what *they* are doing instead of keeping focused on what *we* should be doing.

Thomas Merton said in *No Man Is an Island*, "A selfish love seldom respects the rights of the beloved to be an autonomous person. Far from respecting the true being of another and granting his personality room to grow and expand in its own original way, this love seeks to keep him in subjection to ourselves. It insists that he conform himself to us, and it works in every possible way to make him do so. A selfish love withers and dies unless it is sustained by the attention of the beloved . . . We seek to make pets of them, to keep them tame."

Moonflowers have a unique quality in that they bloom open during the night, but most other flowers do not. They take their time, working in concert with the elements to go from seedling to plant to flower. This also happens with the growth of a child. Children develop motor skills, the ability to speak, and the ability to comprehend at vastly different rates. They take their time . . . and so will you. Moving from vibe to manifestation is going to depend on:

1. What you want

2. The level of *samskaras* that might keep you from opening up the boundaries of your perceptual field

3. The amount of work you do to lessen the *samskaras* so that you're able to line up

The work is to stay mindful and present so that we can go against the grain of our conditioning. And that only happens when we stay present in our own experience and stop concerning ourselves with what others are creating. Instead of getting caught up in the competitive mentality of looking at others, use the evidence of what they are creating as proof that your perceptual field is opening and the *contrast* their experience is showing you as an opportunity to refine and recommit to what you're vibing on. For example, Anna is trying to manifest better health in her life. As she looks at those around her who are healthy and capable of doing things currently unavailable to her, she feels the heaviness of envy weighing on her shoulders. Since she is learning how to vibe, she reaches into her Vibrational Emergency Management Kit and employs a method that calms her down easily, taking ten long breaths. From this calmer place, she explores what it is that other people are experiencing that she'd like to draw into her experience, including the ability to move easily and to be free from pain and medication. As she imagines how life will be with these qualities, she feels better. And as she feels more and more realigned with great health, she realizes that what she's seeing around her is actually evidence that she's getting closer and closer to where she'd like to be. And then she's thankful for the contrast that she experienced . . . it gave her yet another opportunity to show herself just how quickly and easily she can soothe herself back to a great-feeling place.

So . . . mind your own business!

> *One day you finally knew*
>
> *what you had to do, and began,*
>
> *though the voices around you*
>
> *kept shouting*
>
> *their bad advice—*
>
> *though the whole house*
>
> *began to tremble*

and you felt the old tug

at your ankles.

"Mend my life!"

each voice cried.

But you didn't stop.

You knew what you had to do,

though the wind pried

with its stiff fingers

at the very foundations—

though their melancholy

was terrible.

It was already late

enough, and a wild night,

and the road full of fallen

branches and stones.

But little by little,

as you left their voices behind,

the stars began to burn

through the sheets of clouds,

as there was a new voice,

which you slowly

recognized as your own,

that kept you company

as you strode deeper and deeper

into the world,

the only thing you could do—

determined to save

the only life you could save

  ~ Mary Oliver, "The Journey"

For Today:

1. Continue with meditation.

2. For consideration: Is there someone in your life with whom you feel a
    sense of competition? Try to identify what it is about their experience that
    causes you to focus attention on them. It may be that their experience is
    showing you something that bothers you because it's not in line with what
    you are trying to create. If that is the case, recognize this as contrast and
    use it to reaffirm your own vibe. If it is not showing you contrast, then can
    you see that what you perceive is actually evidence that what you are look-
    ing to create is possible and that you are on your way?

Supplemental information, support and community for vibers can be found
online at www.vibeathon.com.

Remember, what you perceive you receive . . . Now, vibe on!

Day Twenty: Hula Dancing Flamingoes

If you can see your path laid out in front of you step by step, you know it's not your path.

Your own path you make with every step you take. That's why it's your path.

~ Joseph Campbell

A number of years ago on a nephew's fourth birthday, he and his cousins spent the afternoon at a store dedicated to creating individualized stuffed animals. Later on in the celebration I met up with the group—all were eager to show me their creations. There was a dog dressed as a fireman, a flamingo dressed as a hula dancer, a frog costumed as Spider Man, and more. Each one was a perfectly unique and individual masterpiece, as well as a superlative representation of its creator.

Never once did these wonderful little beings think it was strange to create a chipmunk cheerleader or an iguana army fighter. Nor did they ask anyone if it was *right* or *appropriate* to bring into reality what they created from their imaginations. They simply fashioned what was interesting for them . . . what they desired.

When I looked at the eight magnificent creations lined up on the couch, I realized that this is what it's all about. It's about allowing ourselves to be blue bear football players and to create ballerina cows without hesitation or the slightest thought that it might be inappropriate or wrong, or that there may even be a more "right" way to create.

Because there isn't a right way to create anything!

What is it that keeps us from fully expressing ourselves creatively, or holds us back from lining up with what we want? As much as we may want to manifest something, when it really comes down to it we often butt up against some level of resistance. And this mental—or *thought-inspired* resistance can become either a small pebble or a mile-high-and-mile-wide boulder that holds us back.

What gives?

The resistance that we encounter is often based on fear : fear that we can't have what we want, or fear that we won't be supported and therefore validated in what we have created.

FEAR = *False Expectations Appear Real*

And yes, they appear real, because that is what we perceive. We focus on what we fear instead of what we want!

Fear is one of the major obstacles that keep us on the path of external reaching (trying to force something to happen) and off the path of internal seeking (which includes vibing). As mentioned in week one, these obstacles are known in the Yoga Sutras as the *klesas*. To review:

— We human beings have thoughts.

— Thoughts we think over and over become habitual patterns of thought (*samskaras*).

— *Samskaras* that become so ingrained that they appear as full-on representations of our personality are *klesas*.

Abhinivesa, the fifth *klesa*, is often defined as fear. In a more accurate translation, *abhinivesa* is clinging to bodily life. When there is major identification with the physical as all there is, fear will ensue.

Fear is the product of the granddaddy of all the *klesas*, *avidya*. *Avidya* is ignorance of what's real; it's the belief that we are our thoughts, our body, this physical presence. If we believe that this is all there is, of course we're going to cling. Right? Who wouldn't?

But we're not THIS! What we really are is that eternal, limitless miracle that resides in but is not part of the body. The more we can tune in to THAT—to our true Self—the more secure we become within ourselves. The more secure we are the less we need external validation or support for our choices. And then the possibilities for creating become endless.

When we are children we have creative experiences over and over. These experiences become part of the conditioning that determines our personalities and how we label ourselves through the ego. The ego is where we come up against resistance as adults. It is about control, keeping us confined within the boundaries of the perception that it continues to define for us, based on the previous conditioning and experiences that may not be so conducive to creating something new. Learning how to be creative when we are adults requires that we transcend the ego conditioning, that we move beyond the boundaries of our previous experiences and open up to the unlimited realm of possibilities. We accomplish this by clearing the space and training the mind to do our bidding in meditation, and then continuing the work of reconditioning through daily mindfulness—learning how to be less reactive in order to make choices that are in line with what we are looking to create and not in line with what we fear.

The gray matter of the brain is largely composed of the cell bodies of neurons. And they are all there, at the ready to forge new synapses in the form of patterns of thought for us to create what we want—to get away from the limiting *samskaras* and *klesas* mentioned previously and to create new neural pathways that are consistent with where we want our minds, and therefore our lives, to go. But we have to do the work of repatterning our thoughts through continual, conscious effort. The only things in life that are unavailable to us are the things that we deem so. It's as simple as that.

If the kids had lined up eight identical stuffed bears on the couch that day, can you imagine how boring and uninspired that would have been? And the reality is, the individuality of those stuffed animals led to a level of playfulness and further imagination and creativity between the children that will only foster more enthusiasm to create.

What joy to see such wonderful, crazy, colorful expressions of the vibrational process coming to fruition. In my humble opinion, that is absolute joy . . . that is life at its fullest . . . and hula dancing flamingos totally rock!

Two roads diverged in a yellow wood,

And sorry I could not travel both

And be one traveler, long I stood

And looked down one as far as I could

To where it bent in the undergrowth;

Then took the other, as just as fair,

And having perhaps the better claim,

Because it was grassy and wanted wear;

Though as for that the passing there

Had worn them nearly about the same,

And both that morning equally lay

In leaves no step had trodden black.

Oh, I kept the first for another day!

Yet knowing how way leads on to way,

I doubted if I should ever come back.

I shall be telling this with a sigh

Somewhere ages and ages hence:

Two roads diverged in a wood, and I—

I took the one less traveled by,

And that has made all the difference.

~ Robert Frost, "The Road Not Taken"

For Today:

1. Continue with meditation.

2. For consideration: Is there a fear element attached to the subject of your Vibe-a-Thon? Is there a part of you that is afraid of the choice that you've made and whether or not other people will accept it? If so, take a little time today and create a vision where everything has come into place and you are sharing what you've created with others. In your vision, see the others as supportive and excited.

Supplemental information, support and community for vibers can be found online at www.vibeathon.com.

Remember, what you perceive you receive . . . Now, vibe on!

Day Twenty-one: It's Time to Talk about TIME

Imagine: You are sitting in a room with the sound of a clock ticking.

Ticking . . .

Ticking . . .

Like the stopwatch from *60 Minutes*, it's loud enough to hear. As the announcer describes the evening's stories, the stopwatch ticks away in the background, the ever-present reminder that, with time, the show will end.

I've been thinking a lot about time lately, especially in terms of the limits or boundaries we place on what we are working toward manifesting. And you see it constantly—someone is hoping to have or achieve something within a specific period of time:

"I want to make a million dollars by the time I'm forty."

"I want to be married by the time I'm twenty-eight."

"I will own a successful business within two years."

"I will finish writing the book in four months."

Is the vision of what you want to create being held prisoner by time?

What is time, anyway? Is it an actual thing, or something that humans have created in order to have some semblance of structure within society? Physicists and philosophers have looked at the concept of time for centuries, and continue to debate both its validity and relevance.

"In book 11 of *Confessions*, as part of an argument which anticipates the theory of relativity, Augustine points out that the three divisions of time have no independent, absolute existence. What we call past, present, and future are really only three ways that human consciousness orients itself to phenomena: recollection, awareness, anticipation. Consciousness itself, or God, has absolute existence and is altogether beyond time."[34]

Time as we know it was born in Greenwich, England, in 1884 when a world conference decided that the meridian line that passes through the observatory there would be the initial meridian . . . the master time for the planet. GMT is our best approximation of time as defined by Sir Isaac Newton. As attributed to Newton, the universe is like a large clock, set into motion by God and keeping absolute time behind the scenes. In this view, that universal clock keeps on keeping on, regardless of what's happening within the universe. However, in modern times Albert Einstein blew that theory apart, stating that time is created by the relationships of the changes that happen in the universe as the basis of his theory of relativity.

On top of that, add in the fact that our perception of time is governed by biological and psychological states and can be altered by such means as sensory deprivation, overstimulation, and altered states of consciousness. As stated by David Eagleman of the Baylor College of Medicine, "What we're learning in neuroscience is that time is not what we thought it was. It's not something you're passively tracking—instead, it's something you're actively constructing with the brain. And my brain and your brain can be very different in terms of how they see the same event."[35]

This is yet another reason why meditation is so important. In the practice of meditation, we can literally slow down our perception of time, as well as quell our need for something to happen within a certain period of time.

What if time is really nothing more than a stubborn psychological filter? When you really think about it, it's enough to blow your mind . . . or at least your concept of time!

Do you have a time limit for the subject of your Vibe-a-Thon? Why? When we set ourselves within the boundary of time, i.e., "I want to manifest this by *x*,"

---

34   Eknath Easwaran, *The Upanishads*, p. 57
35   "Does Time Exist," *Through the Wormhole*, Science Channel, June 22, 2011

what we are actually offering vibrationally is that we don't really believe that this will ever happen, so we'll play the game of vibing but when the deadline hits, the doubts our ego has created to keep control will have proven correct. Because, in fact, you are lined up with the doubt and so that is what you will continue to perceive evidence of and find opportunity to create more of.

Wow. That's a really ineffective way for us to validate ourselves, isn't it? And yet that's what most of us do, because we are still living unconsciously. We haven't trained our minds to do our bidding, so the ego runs amok. And we're left unfulfilled when our deadline arrives.

You don't know how things are going to play out. And how long it takes for your vision to manifest is dependent both on how lined up you are and on your ability to let go of the time in which you feel it needs to happen. For when we are in a state of Oneness and knowing that we are in the process of creating— and both present and inspired within that process—it's almost as though time does not exist. We have all had experiences where we're so focused on what we are doing that we don't realize we've been at it for hours. That's what you need with the subject of your Vibe-a-Thon.

I was a professional singer when I was in my twenties. For ten years in the dive bars of Manhattan, I made my way from backup singer to lead vocalist to head of my own band. During that time I was a little babe in the woods as far as vibing was concerned—could see as clearly as daylight that I would one day be onstage in front of thousands of people, but didn't know enough about the subtleties of this work to realize that I had begun to hold my vision from my ego's drive for validation and from the need to get "there" (wherever "there" was) as soon as possible—not from the joy of the work. And at the end of those ten years, I was burnt out from the effort and had long ago left the joy behind.

That was a beautiful and important lesson for me. As I dedicated myself more and more to the study of yoga and to deepening of my yoga practice and to teaching, I made sure (and continue to make sure) that I stayed on the path of joy. To stay interested in what I do and to act in service to those with whom I share what I have come to understand. And here's the interesting thing: a few years ago, I was presented with the opportunity to be onstage in Central Park for what was hailed as the largest gathering of yoga ever. Was I singing? Sure,

I chanted. But I also kept my eyes wide open, so I could drink in something I had set into motion years before. As I looked out at the thousands of people, what gave me the greatest delight was a small group of students who had made their way to the stage. They were in training with me and thrilled to see their teacher on stage. Realizing that I truly cared more about those perky beings than about gaining any thrill from a crowd was the truest sense of validation I could have received, and the clearest indication of how not getting caught up in the details of time can lead you to where your heart's desire is.

Hold on to your vision, but let go of the parameters. Because you never know—what's in store may be so much more than you could come up with on your own, if you just give it time.

For Today:

1. Continue with meditation.

2. For consideration: Try the following exercise.

    Ask yourself: "Where am I?"

    Answer: "Here."

    Ask yourself: "What time is it?"

    Answer: "Now."

    Say it until you can actually hear it.

Supplemental information, support and community for vibers can be found online at www.vibeathon.com.

Remember, what you perceive you receive . . . Now, vibe on!

Week Four

As the sun, who is the eye of the world,

Cannot be tainted by the defects in our eyes

Nor by the objects it looks on,

So the one Self, dwelling in all, cannot

Be tainted by the evils of the world.

For this Self transcends all! (Katha Upanishad II.2.11)[36]

Welcome to week four. You've spent the past weeks learning that all reality is perceived. You've identified the subject of your individual Vibe-a-Thon and set intentions to allow both evidence of and opportunity for its fruition. You have started the process of opening perception by resculpting your previous patterns of conditioning and thoughts through the process of meditation and mindfulness in daily life. You have come to view the not-so-great stuff as nothing more than contrast allowing you to further clarify exactly what you want. You've identified where you are on the vibrational spectrum as well as how to move toward what you are looking to create in your life, and you've stockpiled your Vibrational Emergency Management Kit so that you have plenty of tools for those times when your vibing gets a little wonky.

You're vibing . . . you're vibing . . . and now?

Now, you ALLOW IT IN. And I know, that sounds simplistic. But it's where many experience a final level of resistance that holds manifestation at bay, until they learn how to allow.

How good are you at allowing? As the evidence of your desired manifestation begins to present itself in the form of new ideas and opportunities, what is your reaction? Does manifestation feel like the next logical step? Does it freak you out? Do you try to convince yourself that it's a fluke and you had a lucky moment but things will soon return to "normal"? Or have you slipped back

36   Eknath Easwaran, *The Upanishads*, p. 94

into the older, established patterns we habitually rely on when we have something we would like to manifest in our lives—have you begun to focus more on the *action* of trying to make something happen and completely let go of the internal process that is so important to vibing? In other words, are you beginning to pressure yourself into forcing something to happen instead of holding your vision, allowing the time for your field of perception to open wide enough to include the evidence and opportunities that feel appropriate and right for you, and *then* taking action?

Don't get me wrong: we are meant to create here on this earth. So, yes, doing is important. But doing without vibing? That's not so much fun. And it's really unproductive.

When I began to write this chapter, I sat down at the small table I have on my deck, with all my flowers and ivy and 56th Street down below. My cats came out to join me and I experienced how lucky I was to have the space, and those two perfect little creatures to share it. I took out the notebook where I had scribbled down the things I wanted to share for week four. I turned on the computer. I stared at the blank screen. I typed a word . . . and erased it . . . then looked down at the street . . . then looked at the cats . . . then the flowers . . . then got agitated . . . then looked back at the blank screen. I did this for approximately two hours, all the while getting more and more frustrated that the words on the page seemed nothing more than forced bits of verbal vomit that made me wince when I reread them. And I knew everything I wanted to write, but there was something going on inside of me that was simply not letting me reach my ideas.

I wasn't allowing. I was trying so hard to *make it happen* that there was no flow to my work. And I could feel it. So I did the best thing I could: stepped away from the computer, dug into my Vibrational Emergency Management Kit for the perfect tool (a few hours of hang time with my friend up on her roof) and vibed on sitting down at the computer the next morning with a free flow of words and concepts coming out of me.

So far . . . so good!

It's easy to get out of the flow of allowing. And because we have perhaps lived with the belief that things are created externally, by some force or creature or condition outside of ourselves instead of *within* us, that belief is usually where we go when we begin to step out of the flow of allowing and into the state of mind where we feel like we can have only by actively making it happen.

As evidence of manifestation begins to present itself, it's not uncommon to try to fit it within the confined mental constructs we have created through the course of our lives. When the blinders begin to peel back through the process of mindfulness and meditation—and as the evidence, new ideas, and opportunities start to peek through—the ego is going to do everything in its power to snap those blinders back into place. As they once again restrict our field of vision, we move into the narrowing spiral of judgment and out of the spaciousness of curiosity where we're able to glimpse what's new.

What we are allowing in is unfamiliar to the ego. And the synapses that are reinforcing the new thought patterns associated with this exciting, great stuff are akin to weak little muscles. Without internal reinforcement they cannot take hold, and we revert back to our old habits of thought. Which, more often than not, takes us totally out of the place of trusting within, and full-on into looking to some external factor for direction and hope.

Why is it so easy for us to look to outside sources in an effort either to validate the conditions of our lives or to give credit for the things that we, in fact, can and do create for ourselves?

We are the products of tremendously vast influences—religious, cultural, educational, socioeconomic, and familial—the list goes on and on. Underlying those influences is the inherent negative bias that humans live with, based on our predisposition to survive and on the fact that negative emotions dominate us for the most part because we, as a species, never really completed the job of hardwiring positive emotional brain circuits. So positivity and optimism are not as automatic as negative reactions. These influences have, in effect, fitted us with blinders that limit our field of perception and put up boundaries that pen in our creative expression.

We can look at creativity and our propensity for allowing—or the lack thereof—in terms of the gunas, the three qualities of matter and energy that underlie all things in nature.

It is the three gunas born of prakriti—sattva, rajas, and tamas—that bind the immortal Self to the body.

Sattva—pure, luminous, and free from sorrow—binds us with attachment to happiness and wisdom.

Rajas is passion, arising from selfish desire and attachment. These bind the Self with compulsive action.

Tamas, born of ignorance, deludes all creatures through heedlessness, indolence and sleep.

Sattva binds us to happiness; rajas binds us to action. Tamas, distorting our understanding, binds us to delusion.

Sattva predominates when rajas and tamas are transformed. Rajas prevails when sattva is weak and tamas overcome. Tamas prevails when rajas and sattva are dormant.

When sattva predominates, the light of wisdom shines through every gate of the body.

When rajas dominates, a person runs about pursuing selfish and greedy ends, driven by restlessness and desire.

When tamas is dominant a person lives in darkness—slothful, confused, and easily infatuated. (The Bhagavad Gita 14.5–14.13)[37]

When we are in the experience of sattva there is clarity, trust, and absolute allowing. In sattva, we are here and clear. It is within this open, allowing state that the most original, fresh, and imaginative acts of creation take place, and we are truly vibing. The rajasic state is a frenetic, caffeinated, action mode. When we are rajasic, it's like we're trying to beat a square peg into a round hole—we compulsively try to make something happen. Creativity in the rajasic state is more in line with looking to re-create something we already have because the field of perception is limited to what is currently known. The tamasic state is, quite simply,

---

37   Eknath Easwaran, *The Bhagavad Gita*, p. 213

like being stuck in the mud. This is where we get trapped within our previous conditioning and memories, and experience an inability to create.

With both the rajasic and tamasic states there is no real room for allowing, for in the rajasic state we are in too compulsive a state of doing and in the tamasic state we are too dull.

As conscious, present beings we can't knock rajas or tamas because they are a part of nature. And we can't completely denigrate their inherent limitations and boundaries, because they are necessary for all of us! Those forces, both within us and outside of us are the things that show us contrast. And by showing us the contrast of what *doesn't* work for us, they help us to discern what *will* work and then we can begin to vibe on creating that. And the people you know who might read this material on vibration and say it's gobbledygook need this information to be around as well—because it shows *them* the contrast of what *doesn't* resonate for them and brings them to what *does*. And that's cool, as there are as many individual ways to create as there are individuals.

We have elements in life that either show us evidence that we are moving in the right direction or contrast through what is not in line with what we desire; these elements aid us in defining the choices we make. So how do we use what we need effectively without getting mired in the mud of what we don't need? We get focused. We stay conscious and nonreactive. We sift through what we don't like or want or need and find those nuggets that work for us. We hold onto those nuggets and pat ourselves on the back for having found them. And then we open to the realization that there is no such thing as good or bad. There is only the evidence and contrast laid out on the path to help us navigate.

Life can only become what we want if we stay conscious—conscious of what we perceive in terms of the external influences and of *what it is inside of us that is holding us in that perception* so that we can do the work of clearing up those thought patterns and get back in sync.

We live in a world where the philosophical proclivity seems to have moved away from "I am That I am" to the media saturation we can identify as "I REVEAL, therefore I am." We have unlimited external influences available to us twenty-four hours a day, seven days a week. Through modern gadgetry, we are instantaneously made aware of large cultural incidents as well as the latest accomplishments of family and friends. If we are not in the active practice of staying present and non-reactive to the wealth of information coming in, it will take us directly out of vibing and into a preoccupation with external reaching, leading to imbalance in the lower three chakras. Within the Manipura chakra (solar plexus) this imbalance will display as the pursuit of power and dominance; in the Svadisthana chakra (sacral region), imbalance appears as the pursuit of sensual pleasure; and in the Muladhara chakra (pelvic floor), it manifests as the pursuit of stuff.

But it's not just the big external (i.e., societal, cultural) influences that we need to see clearly! It's small gatherings of people talking on any subject that often have more of an influence on where you land on the vibrational spectrum.

When we are out of the balance and clarity of vibing that is sattva, we move either into the compulsive drive for action that is rajas or into the dullness that is tamas. This is the danger zone, for when we stop looking within for support and direction, the only alternative is to look to others. Those around us can be an amazing source of support and strength, but beware! They are the culmination of their own conditioning, experiences, and memories. And as we know, their individual walls of perception are limited to that culminated extent.

If a pickpocket meets a saint, he sees only his pockets.

~ Hari Dass Baba

Are your friends truly looking out for what it is that you want in your life, or are they advising you in a fashion that validates *their* experience? No, they're not out to get you, and it's not something that they necessarily do consciously. If they have not yet learned to vibe, they are simply in the cycle of playing their usual reactive tapes—receiving a stimulus and trying to create the response that will leave *them* vindicated. This is nothing more than unconscious human nature. And so, you need to make sure that the way they are advising or supporting you is in *your* best interest, not theirs. You must make sure that you sift through their words, clear away the bits that are offered from behind their veils of fear and competition and get to the evidence and contrast that will continue to help you navigate. In doing so, you become the example to them of conscious, nonreactive, active creating.

One morning, I walked through Central Park to teach my class at a West Side studio. Entering the park at the bottom of the lower loop, I walked against the combined flow of automobile traffic, runners, and bikers. As the vehicles and people made their way past me, I took in little things about some of them . . . others passed by without notice. I allowed everything and everyone to entertain me during my walk, but kept moving toward my destination.

Interestingly, not once did I think to myself that I should be moving in the same direction as the vast majority. It was never even a thought. I knew where I was going . . . knew the path that would lead me there . . . and kept on it.

As you work toward manifesting those things you desire in your life, are you able to stay on your path *regardless* of what others may say or think? Or do you change direction—and thereby change your focus—in order to be part of their flow?

We have not come here to take prisoners,

But to surrender ever more deeply

To freedom and joy.

We have not come into this exquisite world

To hold ourselves hostage from love.

Run my dear,

From anything

That may not strengthen

Your precious budding wings.

Run like hell, my dear,

From anyone likely

To put a sharp knife

Into the sacred, tender vision

Of your beautiful heart.

We have a duty to befriend

Those aspects of obedience

That stand outside of our house

And shout to our reason

"Oh please, oh please,

Come out and play."

We have not come here to take prisoners

Or to confine our wondrous spirits,

But to experience ever and ever more deeply

Our divine courage, freedom and light!

~ Hafiz[38]

On day nine, we looked at sutra 1.33 and saw how it can help us find peace within as we negotiate our relationships with those around us. Cultivating

---

38   Daniel Ladinsky, *The Gift: Poems by Hafiz, The Great Sufi Master*, p. 28

attitudes of friendliness/kindness toward those who are happy, compassion for those who are less fortunate, delight in the virtuous, and equanimity toward those whose actions oppose our values are the keys to letting go of much of the need for external reaching in daily life. Consider, as well:

—   Every individual is the radiant, immortal, infinite light and goodness inside, but that light is covered with different layers and shadings that are the product of their lives.

—   It is the reactions within our own minds that create suffering in response to the actions of others.

—   Peace of mind comes from within when we calm the thoughts and reactions.

—   When we are open and calm in the mind, the blinders peel away and our perception opens up to move beyond the disparaging thoughts about others and toward that which we are looking to create.

I remember a situation from college that perfectly describes the external-influence danger zone. I lived on a dorm floor with around forty other girls. One day, one of the girls on the floor received a card from her on-again, off-again boyfriend. In the card, he described how deeply he cared for her, but said it was time for them to go their separate ways because a long-distance relationship wasn't going to work for him and they were too young to be tied down to something that didn't work very well anyway. He hoped that she was open to remaining friends.

When I saw her studying in the lounge, she didn't seem upset. She actually felt the same way that he did, and was somewhat relieved to think that they could really be friends. She seemed OK with it.

OK with it . . . until the rest of the girls on the dorm floor got wind of it, that is!

I saw her in the elevator a day or so after she received the card. She looked angry and determined, and when I asked her what was up, she handed me an envelope that she was about to seal. "Read this," she said "I'm so proud of myself!"

I read the letter, addressed to her now ex-boyfriend and spewing so much anger and venom that it could have stung my fingers. I asked her where the sudden change of heart came from, and she responded that she thought she was OK . . . until she spoke with the other girls on our dorm floor.

She related that some of the girls found out about the card. And these girls not only counseled her on how she *really* should be feeling about it . . . not only did they talk her into writing a letter back . . . they wrote the letter for her! Can you imagine the wrath of some twenty hormonal young girls, gathering their collective frustrated expectations about love and relationships (and the resultant battle scars) and putting it down on paper?

Yes, that's a fairly dramatic and somewhat immature example of the power of a group. And, as we age, things soften but do they change completely? Does that mean we have to let go of all of our friends in order to be vibers? No, of course not. But we have to selectively sift through what is being said around us, and discard those not-so-shiny nuggets that we know, in our hearts, are not in line with what we're looking to create.

Those same groups of people offer a great opportunity to see where we are on our vibrational spectrum. Ever notice that when you're feeling out of sorts with money, you seem to find one, two, or twelve people who are experiencing the same thing? When you're trying to find more time to exercise, you suddenly find that everyone is having the same issue?

Try cleaning up your vibration a bit, and notice how things change!

It's important to bear in mind that *you create your own reality*. Nobody else does. Oh, sure, other people can make suggestions or try to influence you, but it is always your choice to follow an influence or not. And when you get to the place where you truly understand that *what you perceive you receive*, you will no longer permit the words of others to sway you from the good-feeling thoughts that bring you into vibrational sync. You will have taken charge of your life. It's as simple as that.

With all this in mind, how do we stay in the flow of allowing?

Keep the vision of what you are creating. Stay focused on what you want and know that you are entitled to whatever that is. Look at all the people who have created masterfully. Can you imagine if Thomas Edison looked at the oil lamps on his desk and said, "Oh well, this is all there is"? Or if Gandhi believed the conditions within his country were impossible to change? Or if—heaven forbid—Elvis asked his friends if he should sing the crazy new music called rock and roll and then listened to them as they counseled him to learn to play the oboe? All of them held their focus on their vision of what they wanted, *not on what they currently perceived as reality*. And when the things they worked to manifest started coming in, they didn't run away and hide. They rode the wave, allowing and believing the evidence that they were on their way.

Stay in a place of curiosity—not judgment—regarding opportunities that come your way. Let's say Larry is vibing on writing the next great American novel, but he needs inspiration. He is walking down the street and holding his vision of receiving inspiration to start him off. "I need something to start me off. Please, anything to get me going!" A minute later, he sees a really large man walking down 6th Avenue. He's got an evident five o'clock shadow, is wearing a very ornate angel costume with a halo, carrying a six-pack, and has a lit cigarette dangling from his mouth. (I actually did see this once. I love NYC.) However crazy it may seem, Larry *obviously* just received an opportunity . . . but will he take it? And, again, that's a slightly comical example. But the fact is that once you start to open the field of perception, opportunities will show up. And the opportunity may seem small and even insignificant, but it may get you started on your path, and toward the opportunity that will be significant. If you use it.

Heed the contrast. You will always know exactly where you are on your vibrational spectrum through your emotions. When you start to feel a bit funky, you are getting out of alignment. You're getting out of the flow of allowing. When this happens, stop and acknowledge what's going on. Ask yourself *"Do I want more of this?"* and then get to work, moving back onto the path. You have the tools . . . but they won't do you any good if you don't use them.

Have patience! How long it takes for your vision to manifest is dependent on how lined up you are. And, depending on the strength of the disallowing beliefs holding you at bay, it may take a little time. If it is not yet manifest in your life, it simply means you need to continue with the work of vibing. As you find your alignment and hold it, you need to have patience. Because it may be 60 per-cent manifest, or 85 percent manifest. And you have to keep doing the work in order for it to be 100 percent.

It's like waiting for the subway. You make it down onto the platform and look to the tunnel to see if the train is coming, spotting a dim light in the distance. Do you say, "Oh, it's not here so I guess I'll walk"? Well, you might, but that would be silly. Of course you don't—you see the light, you know the train is coming, but you have to allow it to fully arrive at the station.

There's a second aspect of patience here—and it's possibly more important than any other piece to this wonderful puzzle. Have patience with *yourself*! All of these tools and techniques are things that you've known about forever, but haven't necessarily utilized in any consistent, concrete way. And in the same way that you would never chastise a baby for not walking perfectly the first time it takes hesitant steps, neither should you reprimand yourself for the baby steps you're taking toward creating your life. You'll get there! The more you practice the techniques the easier it will become. But allow for the learning. Al-low for the baby steps as you hold your vision, as you learn how to allow.

Exercises for Week Four

Exercise #1: Noticing how people take (or don't take) a compliment is a great way to understand how people work with or against the flow of allowing in their own lives.

1. During the course of the week, compliment ten people. Notice their reactions. Are they accepting and allowing? Or is the compliment met with a justification or an excuse?

2. Notice your reaction as you receive a compliment. Do you take it in, or is there resistance to it? If there's resistance, replay the conversation in your head and see if you can soften so that you graciously accept the praise.

Exercise #2: Are you flowing with the evidence?

Spend the week collecting evidence of the subject of your Vibe-a-Thon manifesting in your life. Notice and write down your own *reaction* to the evidence. Are you resisting the evidence? Trying to do something about it (i.e., force the issue or make it happen)? Or are you having fun with the flow?

Exercise #3: Other People!

Pay conscious attention to the conversations that you are partaking in. Can you tell where your vibe is by the general tones of the conversations? Can you sift through the contrasting elements and get to things that will help you on your path as you discard the things that won't?

Meditation: The Session

1. 5 minutes—Alternate Nostril Breathing (i.e., *Nadi Shodhana*)

2. 5 minutes—Breath Awareness

3. 15–20 minutes—Effortful Concentration (*Dharana*)

4. 5–7 minutes—Visualization

Supplemental information, support and community for vibers can be found online at www.vibeathon.com.

Remember, what you perceive you receive . . . Now, vibe on to week four!

Day Twenty-three: Should You Stay or Should You Go?

What if what you are looking to create isn't coming into fruition? Should you keep honing the vibe or let it go? When is it the right time to let it go, to give up? We've discussed the necessity of *vairagya* in yoga—nonattachment or letting go.

So, should you stay or should you go?

These are questions that often come up after a few weeks of vibing, and raise good issues to contemplate.

First, you need to gauge exactly where you are on our vibrational spectrum. Specifically, where you truly are—with both your thoughts and emotions—in association with where you want to be. When you think about the subject of your Vibe-a-Thon:

- Is there a natural feeling of expectation or does it feel forced?

- Are you aligned with what you're vibing on to the extent that there's a sense of belief, faith, and trust that you're on the right path?

- Is your thinking in line with what you are looking to create, but you're unable to get to the feelings that support those thoughts?

- Or . . . when you think of this thing, are you solely focused on the fact that you don't have it yet? Are you so caught up in a trap of accumulating evidence *against* what you're vibing on that your field of perception can't open up to show you anything new?

Sutra 1.41, one of the most beautiful in the first pada, or book, states, "Just as the naturally pure crystal assumes shapes and colors of objects placed near it, so the yogi's mind, with its totally weakened modifications, becomes clear and balanced and attains the state devoid of differentiation between knower, knowable and knowledge. This culmination of meditation is *samadhi*."

When we are in a state of clarity in the mind, the blinders restraining our current perception peel away and we open to realize endless evidence of and opportunity for the creation we desire. When the thoughts, *samskaras*, and *klesas* are weakened, the grip of doubt and the lack of confidence loosen. What remains is the understanding that all things are possible to the extent that we believe they are possible. From that place we are able to discern clearly the appropriate action to take. The more peace we attain in our minds, the more consciously we are able to create our lives. Conversely, when we are focused on thoughts that lead us down the deep, dark path of disallowing beliefs, our perception can show us only those *limits* as reality—and we stay within the restrictions we have created for ourselves.

It's an absolutely natural part of the process to come up against reactions such as *It's not going to work*; *I'm no good at this*; *There must be something better I can vibe on*; or the ever-popular *This doesn't work for me*. But before giving up, take a look at where your thoughts are. Are you thinking about what you are looking to create, or what you have previously perceived from your years of conditioning? Are you looking at where you're going or at where you have been?

One evening, I sat on a large chair in my living room, with my cat Wilma curled up sleeping next to me. She simultaneously stretched, woke up, and gave a piercing yelp. I looked down and saw that as she stretched she was unintentionally stabbing one of her paws with a claw from her other paw. When I plucked the claw out, the look on her face made it clear she had no idea what had just happened.

In a similar way, how often do the subliminal thoughts that result from a lifetime of conditioning keep us from moving forward in our lives?

Remember, this is not magic and luck has absolutely nothing to do with it! It's easy to fantasize about what we'd like to have in life, but vibing and creating is an actual practice. We have identified that practice must be consistent, must take place over a long period of time, and must be pursued with passion (sutra 1.14) . In addition, the time necessary for success depends on whether the practice is mild, medium, or intense (sutra 1.22) . It's not a question of whether this works for you or not. Rather, the question is this: Are you willing to do the internal work that vibing and creating require?

Lastly, we need to consider just how true and strong the desire is. Through the process of the Vibe-a-Thon, some arrive at a state of clarity in understanding that what they were seeking to create no longer resonates with them. The path of yoga is one that organically leads us away from external reaching and toward the more harmonious path of inward seeking. During the past weeks we have looked at thoughts and *samskaras* and learned how to soften them through mindfulness and meditation. And so, perhaps the thing you began the Vibe-a-Thon with was merely the catalyst to get you started on understanding yourself. Maybe the subject of your Vibe-a-Thon was *you* all along.

Should you stay or should you go? There is no right or wrong answer, only the choice. And the great thing is that no one makes that determination but you, because you are coming to understand that life isn't something that happens to you. As conscious individuals, we create our lives by taking in the evidence and choosing where we want to go. Based on each choice we make, another set of choices will come up. And the creation continues. How fantastic is that?

For Today:

1.   Continue with meditation.

2.   For consideration: To help figure out if you should stay or go, revisit one of the exercises from the very beginning of the Vibe-a-Thon. Make a list of disallowing statements and things you perceive as holding you back. Then, on a fresh sheet of paper, rewrite each item on the list and next to it create a statement that softens the negativity into a hopeful positive statement. For example:

Statement	BETTER Statement
I'm no good at vibing.	This is completely new to me. It's a new way of thinking, and I never really even tried to meditate before the Vibe-a-Thon. There are lots of things that I felt unsure about in the beginning, but as I kept doing the work I really mastered those things. This should be no different.

Continue with all of the items on your list.

Supplemental information, support and community for vibers can be found online at www.vibeathon.com.

Remember, what you perceive you receive . . . Now, vibe on!

Day Twenty-four: Intellectual Blasphemy, Biology, and Belief

In 1952 a young British physician made a mistake. It was a mistake that was to bring short-lived scientific glory to Dr. Albert Mason. Mason tried to treat a fifteen-year-old boy's warts using hypnosis. Mason, and other doctors had successfully used hypnosis to get rid of warts, but this was an especially tough case. The boy's leathery skin looked more like an elephant's hide than a human's, except for his chest, which had normal skin.

Mason's first hypnosis session focused on one arm. When the boy was in a hypnotic trance, Mason told him that the skin on that arm would heal and turn into healthy, pink skin. When the boy came back a week later, Mason was gratified to see that the arm looked healthy. But when Mason brought the boy to the referring surgeon, who had unsuccessfully tried to help the boy with skin grafts, he learned that he had made a medical error. The surgeon's eyes were wide with astonishment when he saw the boy's arm. It was then that he told Mason that the boy was suffering, not from warts, but from a lethal genetic disease called congenital ichthyosis. By reversing the symptoms using "only" the power of the mind, Mason and the boy had accomplished what had until that time been considered impossible. Mason continued the hypnosis sessions, with the stunning result that most of the boy's skin came to look like the healthy, pink arm after the first hypnosis session. The boy, who had been mercilessly teased in school because of his grotesque-looking skin, went on to lead a normal life.

When Mason wrote about his startling treatment for ichthyosis in the British Medical Journal in 1952, his article created a sensation. Mason was touted in the media and became a magnet for patients suffering from the rare, lethal disease that no one before had ever cured. But hypnosis was in the end not a cure-all. Mason tried it on a number of other ichthyosis patients, but he was never able to replicate the results he had with the young boy. Mason attributes his failure to his own belief about the treatment. When Mason treated the new patients he couldn't replicate his cocky attitude as a young physician thinking he was treating a bad case of warts. After that first patient, Mason was fully aware that he was treating what everyone in the medical establishment knew to be a congenital, "incurable" disease. Mason tried to pretend that he was upbeat about the prognosis, but he told the Discovery Health Channel, "I was acting." (Discovery Health Channel 2003)[39]

More and more, Western medicine and science have been studying the mind/ body connection and its role in health . . . knowledge that is at the heart of what yoga is all about. Derived from the words *ayus* ("life") and *veda* ("knowledge"), Ayurveda is the "science of life," and is often called the sister science of yoga. The practice of Ayurveda is between four thousand and five thousand years old—references to its many applications are found in the Vedas, the earliest philosophical writings on yoga in current existence. Through Ayurveda we explore health and wellness in our lives by first understanding our own individual constitutional nature or *prakriti*, and then learning how to live in harmony with the world around us. Ayurveda offers us an individualized template that, once understood, allows us to make daily choices that can keep us in absolute health and clarity—physically, mentally, emotionally, and spiritually.

One of the great things about Ayurvedic medicine is the cognizance that normality varies from person to person, because each and every individual is absolutely unique. Everything in nature has its dharma, which can be thought of as purpose within the cosmic order. Everything that is manifest is a living expression of nature. When we are in harmony with our internal nature to the point where we are in harmony with all of nature, we experience well-being. Our connection to that which infuses all life is unrestricted and our perceptions of reality are clear.

Daily perception consists of interactions. Our senses (sight, sound, taste, touch, smell) interact with objects (both external and internal) and bring information about the objects to the mind. In turn, the mind carries these perceptions to our intellect. If the mind is sattvic (here and clear), the perceptions are equally as clear and we are free to make choices in line with well-being. More often than not, the mind is clouded by rajasic (agitated) and tamasic (dull) qualities, which lead to misperception of information.

When we are not clear, it is not possible to listen to the body's intelligence. In Ayurveda, this intellectual blasphemy is called *prajnaparadha*. *Prajnaparadha* is responsible for the *klesas* (ignorance, egoism, attachment, aversion, fear) that cloud

---

39   Bruce Lipton, *The Biology of Belief*, p. 93

our perspective and cause us to mistrust our individual knowing. According to Vasant Lad, Master of Ayurvedic Science and one of the premier Ayurvedic doctors in the United States, "Intelligence is the flow of awareness and that flow tells us what we should and should not do. Even when an action is wrong, we often go ahead and do it. By that action, we are insulting the intelligence of the body. That is the beginning of disease, whether it is psychological or physical."[40]

Ayurveda divides the progression of disease into six stages and views *prajnaparadha* as the inception of most diseases. Within the first three of the six stages, we have the full capacity to reverse the course back to health through the power of the mind and by making conscious, active choices. The longer we go without making conscious choices that are in line with what we know we should do, the deeper the disease will manifest. Here's a look at the stages where we can easily come back to health:

Stage One: Imagine that a friend has given you a large box of your favorite chocolates, and though you intended to savor them by allocating one per day, you find that within an hour all that's left is the box. After your stomach settles a bit, you begin to crave something salty. This craving is your intelligence leading you toward the elements that will bring you back into balance. If you make correct, conscious choices, you will be back to normal in no time.

Stage Two: Imagine that the same friend is a food critic for a magazine and is in town for the weekend to research an article on the spiciest Mexican food. He invites you to dinner on Friday night and you eat the spiciest food, the hottest chilies—the whole enchilada. Saturday morning you wake up with a mild feeling of indigestion, but feel OK despite having feasted because it's just that one meal and you can eat lightly now. Then your friend calls and says he had such a great time with you that he wants you to accompany him at all the restaurants he has lined up. Breakfast, lunch, and dinner for the next two days, all spicy, all the time—and you accept. By Sunday night, the acid content of your stomach has maxed out, and you know you need to spend a good few days eating mild food. Again, if you make the correct, conscious choice, you will be back to normal sooner rather than later.

Stage Three: It is the holiday season, and your friend the food critic has moved to town permanently. You spend the first few weeks after Thanksgiving indulging, during

---

40   Vasant Lad, *Textbook of Ayurveda*, p. 9

which time you have developed more of a taste for these things and begin to crave them. Rich foods, cheeses, wines, sweets—by the week before Christmas, you're spending more and more time each day seeking out snacks and treats. It's the holidays! And the ability to hold back has been pushed to the wayside. You have neglected that internal intelligence for a long enough period of time that imbalance in the body is going to start to manifest (most likely in the form of a belly that would make Santa jealous and digestive disturbances). You will need to make a more concerted effort at this stage to bring yourself back to balance, and depending on how much damage you've done, you'll need to exert that effort over a longer period of time.

When we get beyond the third stage of disease, structural changes begin to happen in the body. The deeper those changes, the more irreversible the disease. At that point, only symptoms can be treated to make the individual more comfortable, but full health cannot be realized.

Lipton states, "Thoughts, the mind's energy, directly influence how the physical brain controls the body's physiology. Thought 'energy' can activate or inhibit the cell's function-producing proteins via the mechanics of constructive and destructive interference."[41] The more mindful we become, the more we can make conscious choices in all areas of our lives. So get inside and listen to yourself. Because everything you need is within. And then, there is absolutely nothing beyond your grasp!

Break open your personal self

to taste the story of the nutmeat soul.

These voices come from that

rattling against the outer shell.

The nut and the oil inside

have voices that can only be heard

41   Bruce Lipton, *The Biology of Belief*, p. 95

with another kind of listening.

If it weren't for the sweetness of the nut,

the inner talking, who would ever shake a walnut?

We listen to words

so we can silently

reach into the other.

Let the ear and mouth get quiet,

so this taste can come to the lip.

Too long we've been saying poetry,

talking discourses, explaining the mystery

outloud. Let's try a dumb experiment.

~ *Rumi*, "A Dumb Experiment"[42]

For Today:

1. Continue with meditation.

2. For consideration: What are some of the thoughts and beliefs you hold regarding your health? Is there a history within your family that has led you to follow along down the path of disease? Can you start to see

---

42   Coleman Barks, *The Essential Rumi*, p. 327

yourself as a unique individual who no longer follows the previous patterns of conditioning that others have succumbed to?

Supplemental information, support and community for vibers can be found online at www.vibeathon.com.

Remember, what you perceive you receive . . . Now, vibe on!

Day Twenty-five: The View from Up Here

As discussed on day twenty-three, in continuing the internal work of meditation and the external work of viewing evidence that you are on the right path and taking opportunities that present for you to create, the actual end product that you had in mind in the beginning of the process may have either changed or somehow shifted.

And that is fantastic!

If we take a vacation to New York City, one of the sights we might choose to visit is the Empire State Building. Looking out from the tenth floor of the building, we'll have a limited view—mostly, the buildings across the street and the cars, buses, and people traveling below. Taking the elevator to the fiftieth floor will offer a much broader range of sights. When we finally reach the top, the vantage point will provide the sensation of feeling as though we are on top of the world. From that height the entire city is available for view in all its panoramic glory, as well as the Hudson and East Rivers, the Statue of Liberty, and bridges linking the island to the surrounding areas. A few minutes on an elevator opens us up to a much wider perspective!

It is much the same experience—within—as we traverse more deeply on the path of yoga, mindfulness in our daily life, and meditation. In the beginning of the Vibe-a-Thon, as you made the choice about what you desired, that choice conceivably came from the deeper place inside that is connected to infinite possibility. And from that starting point, it was imperative to reconstruct your field of perception, to open beyond the previous conditioning and *samskaras* imposed by the ego, and to start taking in the evidence of and opportunity for that which you desire.

Sutra 1.4 states that when we are not in a place of Oneness with ourselves, we are identifying with our thoughts. As you have come to understand the workings of the mind and plugged away at the exercises in this book, you may be experiencing for the first time how it feels to have more control over the mind—and over your life. Through your efforts with daily meditation, some of the limiting chatter has settled and the walls of your perception have begun to dissolve. And so, in the same way that going to the higher floors of the Empire State Building will offer much broader views, you can now open to the possibility that what you are looking to create has—like you—begun to evolve.

As action-oriented beings, we have a tendency to look at creating as a linear process. We climb the ladder to success, and put one foot in front of the other. But when we add into the mix the internal work of vibing, how we create actually changes. It looks less like a linear process, and a little more akin to a lava lamp! The substance within the lamp forms an ever-evolving series of shapes that redefine themselves as they make contact with each other and with the surrounding plastic, and morph through the liquid that holds them. Similarly, the more we can learn to stay open to the new and different offerings bestowed upon us through the widened field of perception, the more possible it is for the things we create—and our lives in general—to open beyond our wildest expectations.

Alternatively, if the subject you've chosen for your Vibe-a-Thon seems to have lost some resonance for you, there is the possibility that what you chose came from within the ego limitations you were previously confined to. Perhaps you made your choice from a place of fear—of not really believing that what you, in fact, truly wanted would ever be possible. If that is the case, it's not too late! Bravo for you for opening up beyond your previous limits! From this new place, the world is yours for the taking. You just have to figure out what the new, unlimited, open you is now ready to create.

In either scenario, what is really needed is trust. Trust in yourself, and trust in the process. Vibing is the process of creating, and life is one big creation. Creating is never done—once you finish something, the next thing is in the works. So relax into the process. Trust that it's all good and getting better, and more importantly, know that you can't do this wrong. You are a magnificent individual, and your individual expression is your gift to the world. And the world fully supports you in whatever wonderful thing it is you are creating. So get to it!

Whether it's a symphony or a coal mine, all work is an act of creating and comes from the same source: from an inviolate capacity to see through one's own eyes—which means: the capacity to perform a rational identification—which means: the capacity to see, to connect and to make what had not been seen, connected and made before.

~ Ayn Rand, Atlas Shrugged

For Today:

1. Continue with meditation.

2. For consideration: Trust yourself! Have you moved beyond the limits of what you previously thought was possible? Does the subject of your Vibe-a-Thon no longer resonate? If so, take the day to absorb into the fullness of this new, less limited you. If you have opened yourself up to a perspective that encompasses more than before, what is it that this new you wants to create?

Supplemental information, support and community for vibers can be found online at www.vibeathon.com.

Remember, what you perceive you receive . . . Now, vibe on!

Day Twenty-six: What Goes Up Must Come Down

Everything is energy and that is all there is to it. Match the frequency of the reality you want and you cannot help but get that reality. It can be no other way. This is not philosophy. This is physics.

~ Albert Einstein

We have looked at quantum physics and the dual concepts of upward and downward causation in the process of creating. Upward causation is based on the notion that creation starts at the level of particles, which then join to form atoms, which then join to form molecules, which then join to form cells, which make up the brain—which informs consciousness. This is the path of action, and has been the foundation of scientific theory since the age of reason. With downward causation, creativity and manifestation of what we desire begins with consciousness, specifically with consciousness choosing from its own possibilities. This is in line with the internal work that you have been doing in honing your vibe. As we know, it is the cooperation of these two processes that enables creation.

Everything that has ever been, anything and everything that anyone ever created was energy first, conjured in thought before it was made into reality. And as a desire becomes more rooted as possible within the individual, the perception opens up. Evidence of moving on the right path and opportunities toward creation flood in, and over time that thought becomes reality.

The chakras are spinning vortexes representing areas that receive, assimilate, and express life force energy through the physical, mental, emotional, and spiritual layers of our being. The word *chakra* literally means "wheel," and the seven major ones that are identified in yoga are stacked along a column of energy that spans from the base of the spine to the crown of the head. This energetic superhighway is called *Sushumna Nadi* and is important for vibers. Energy that moves up the *Sushumna Nadi* from the base to the crown can be considered the *Path of Vibing*. From the crown of the head back down is the *Path of Manifestation*.

**PATH OF
MANIFESTATION**

Sahasrara (crown)

Ajna (third eye)

Visuddha (throat)

Anahata (heart)

Manipura (solar plexus)

Svadisthana (pelvis)

Muladhara (root)

**PATH OF
VIBING**

The Path of Vibing

As we have been practicing, the internal work of opening up our fields of perception through meditation and mindfulness makes up the first necessary steps toward achieving a vibe that is in line with what we are looking to create. Here's a look at how that manifests through each of the seven chakras:

—   The *Muladhara chakra* is the root chakra, associated with the element of earth. It governs our physical structure and health and our sense of rootedness, trust, and boundaries. As we begin on the path of vibing, first we recognize what we currently perceive as reality . . . for if we are not in a place of perceiving where we currently stand, how can we figure out what we want to create? So on the Path of Vibing, the Muladhara chakra is what we could call our *starting point*.

—   The *Svadisthana chakra* is located in the sacral region and is associated with the element of water and our sensate exploration of the world around us. In this space, we identify what it is that we would like to create based on what our starting point has shown us. On the Path of Vibing, the Svadisthana chakra is where we *establish an intention*.

— The *Manipura chakra* is located at the solar plexus (the space between the low ribs and the navel), and is associated with the quality of fire. It is literally the sun inside of us. It is where the ego labels us in mundane ways (*I am a woman*; *I have brown hair*) and in more subtle ways (*I am deserving*; *I am undeserving*). This is also where we access strength, courage, and fortitude. On the Path of Vibing, the Manipura chakra is where we find the *courage* to say that we deserve to attain what we have established as our intention, regardless of what our ego (and others) may think.

— *Anahata*, the heart chakra, is the center of the chakra system, and is considered to be the bridge between the lower (more physical) chakras and the upper three (more spiritual) chakras. Identified with the quality of air, it is the place where we both give out and receive in, and where the qualities of compassion, self-acceptance, balance, and love play their part. On the Path of Vibing, the Anahata chakra is where we develop a *compassionate attitude* toward ourselves, especially as we begin to play with the more challenging aspects of consistent practice both in meditation and in mindfulness in our daily lives.

— The *Visuddha chakra* is located at the throat and associated with the quality of space. It is at this point in the chakra line that we begin to move toward the more ethereal qualities within and to examine how those qualities manifest in our lives, as well as to engage in the more subtle work of vibing. The Visuddha is our center of creativity, communication, and truth. On the Path of Vibing, this chakra brings focus to where we truly are on our vibrational spectrum, and requires that we *clear the disallowing beliefs* that are holding us back from moving toward alignment.

— Representing the third eye point, *Ajna chakra* is the place where vision, dreams, imagination, and visualization come into play. It is associated with the quality of light, with the ability to illuminate the path toward creation in our mind. This is where we intuit, where we recognize patterns both in ourselves and in others, and where we can identify those more subtle *samskaras* that are holding us back from what we desire. On the Path of Vibing, the Ajna chakra is where we fully *hone our ability to hold the vision* that is truly in line with what we want and learn to disregard the discordant images that no longer serve us.

— The *Sahasrara chakra* is the crown or fontanel, where we reconnect with the divine, with that space deep within that knows all and is all. Sahasrara chakra is associated "with the element of thought"[43] and it is in this place where we confront the belief systems that may have held us back and where we continue to open up to more than what we currently regard as truth. On the Path of Vibing, this is the culmination of the work of the other chakras. When we fully line up our beliefs so that we arrive at a place of knowing that what we wish to create is the next logical step, then we have done the internal work necessary. *It is here that we are truly vibing.*

Once we have done the work on the Path of Vibing, we are ready to add in the external work to fully create. The Path of Vibing moves us up through both the chakras and the elements associated with them—elements that we can see are lighter in nature the higher we move up the *Sushumna Nadi*. As we move down the Path of Manifestation, we move from thought down to the element of earth, bringing that which we choose to create into full, concrete reality.

The Path of Manifestation

— *Sahasrara chakra*: In experiencing the full sense of connection, trust, and knowing that we are in our vibe in the crown chakra, *the field of perception begins to open wide.* This is the sense of peace, calm, and spaciousness that can be experienced in deeper states of meditation.

— *Ajna chakra*: As the blinders peel away and the field of perception opens, it is like opening the door to a new world. *New ideas, new visions, and new thought processes* begin to unfold, leading you toward finding evidence that you are on the right path and revealing opportunities for you to take steps toward creating.

— *Visuddha chakra*: From the deepening state of knowing and vibing, it becomes easier to *think, speak, and act in line with what you want.* You

43   Anodea Judith, *Eastern Body, Western Mind*, p. 11

begin to see contrast—a shadow representing what you don't want that helps you clarify what you do. And then you communicate your new internal truth to the world.

— *Anahata chakra*: As you reach out toward the opportunities that present themselves and take in the evidence that you are on the right path, there is a greater sense of *self-acceptance* regarding the ups and downs we experience in vibing. It's not a linear process! Plus, in defining our new selves and starting to take action based on that reworked definition, we develop *compassion*—not only for ourselves, but also for those around us who are struggling in their own lives and perhaps uncomfortable with their changing perception of us.

— *Manipura chakra*: As we come up against the boundaries within which the ego may still be trying to hold us, we stay compassionate and open with ourselves but diligent in our work to restructure those disallowing labels. Moreover, we use the *strength* and *fortitude* of the solar plexus to strive toward action, *taking a risk* when opportunity knocks and putting what we know inside to be true into practice out in the world.

— *Svadisthana chakra*: As we come more deeply into reconnection with our true Self, what we were previously looking to create may no longer resonate for us. Or, we may find that we are shifting a bit too deeply back into action mode and have not continued to hone the vibe. The waters of the Svadisthana chakra help us to *continue navigating through our thoughts and emotions*, making changes as necessary and staying true to what we desire or what we have redefined as our desire.

— *Muladhara chakra*: On the Path of Manifestation, this is the culmination. As evidence and opportunities are taken, the fruits of our labors (both internal and external) lead over time to the *full manifestation* of what we have been in the process of creating. Perception has led to reception . . . and to a new reality!

As Einstein said, this is physics. But it's also philosophy. And more than that, it's reality. If you do the internal work, it will lead to the external actions you need to take. We can truly have or be or do anything. But it's not luck and it's not magic. It's work of the most magnificent kind.

For Today:

1. Continue with meditation.

2. For consideration: Where are you—on the Path of Vibing or the Path of Manifestation?

Supplemental information, support and community for vibers can be found online at www.vibeathon.com.

Remember, what you perceive you receive . . . Now, vibe on!

Day Twenty-seven: Do You Still Believe in Miracles?

There are no accidents in this business at all. Accidents are just from where you're looking. To the ego, it looks like it's miracles and accidents. No miracles. No accidents. It's just your vantage point that you're sort of stuck in.

~ Ram Dass, Be Here Now

At the beginning of this journey I posed the question, *Do you believe in miracles?* The US hockey team's 1980 Olympic win was our first example of how clearly lining up with a vision leads to wonderful accomplishments.

But now, after all the work that you have done to define what you want, after undertaking the internal work of meditation and mindful living, and after taking in the evidence and taking on opportunities to bring your desire into manifestation . . . are you still under the assumption that creation occurs through magic or luck or (dare I say) fate? Can we finally take glorious responsibility for everything that we hold as our current reality, and leave magic to those who haven't yet learned how to vibe? Can our enchantment stem from this (perhaps) newfound belief that what we perceive we receive, and that we are the active players in defining our perception and, therefore, our lives?

Buddha said, "In the sky, there is no distinction of east and west; people create distinctions out of their own minds and then believe them to be true." When there is a profound state of Oneness with our thoughts and words, and the field of perception opens, we redefine our beliefs. We create a new reality. And anything to which we give that kind of full attention will come to fruition. This is among the most fundamental laws related to human existence. And to the degree that thoughts, words, and deeds are in conflict with what we are looking to create, we find that is the degree to which we have not yet fully created. It's safe to say our ability to believe is intrinsically linked to our ability to create.

As he describes in his 1984 book *Beyond the Relaxation Response*, Dr. Herbert
Benson was provided the opportunity to both observe and collect scientific
evidence of Tibetan monks' ability to directly effect changes in their bodies
through the power of the mind—specifically, the ability to raise their internal
body temperature while practicing a meditation technique known as gTum-mo
Yoga while exposed to cold weather. "Literally translated, gTum-mo means
'fierce woman'—'fierce' because the warmth is a fire of purification that de-
cisively counteracts ingrained false ideas, and 'woman' because the state is the
source or 'mother' that gives birth to subtler and higher states of mind."[44] The
rise in temperature claimed by the monks is in direct opposition to the normal
bodily response when exposed to cold temperatures.

What did he find? In observing and measuring the body temperatures of three
monks before, during, and after their sessions of meditation, Dr. Benson noted
body temperatures that not only rose (by up to thirteen degrees in one monk's
fingers and in another monk's toes), but the ability to elicit the state as a
conditioned response. Dr. Benson wrote of the third monk, "oddly enough, he
was apparently so attuned to this form of meditation that the physical changes
associated with gTum-mo occurred whenever he sat down, whether he was
trying to meditate or not."[45]

The third chapter of Patanjali's Yoga Sutras, Vibhuti Pada, deals with the accomplishments that come as a result of the yoga practice. Here, Patanjali speaks
of *samyama*, the art of integration through effortful concentration (*dharana*),
effortless concentration/meditation (*dhyana*), and total absorption in one's
true Self (*samadhi*). *Samyama* encompasses the disciplines necessary to live in
the natural grace of yoga, and accounts for the accrual of supernatural powers,
or *siddhis*.[46]

There are remarkable powers listed in this section that seem both unachievable
and downright sensational. And yet, Patanjali assures us that if we are truly in
state of complete and total absorption with what we have set our attention on,
its manifestation is imminent. And though the elements of *samyama* are experienced when we venture toward the deepest states of ourselves, we can look to
them as templates for how to create out in the world. Here are a few:

44   Herbert Benson, *Beyond the Relaxation Response*, p. 48
45   Ibid, p. 59
46   B. K. S. Iyengar, *Light on the Yoga Sutras of Patanjali*, p. 165

3.24 [The yogi] gains moral and emotional strength by perfecting friendliness and other virtues towards one and all.

3.25 By samyama *on strength, the yogi will develop the physical strength, grace, and endurance of an elephant.*

3.27 By samyama *on the sun the yogi will have knowledge of the seven worlds, and of the seven cosmic centers in the body.*

3.28 By samyama *on the moon, the yogi will know the position and system of the stars.*

3.34 Through the faculty of spiritual perception the yogi becomes the knower of all knowledge.

3.35 By samyama *on the region of the heart, the yogi acquires a thorough knowledge of the contents and tendencies of consciousness.*[47]

Wow! These are breathtaking attainments, are they not? How amazing it would be to acquire the strength of an elephant or amass knowledge of all things! Are the *siddhis* really possible? We can't discredit these statements because, unless we have honestly come to that deep a state of absorption, we will never know what is possible. For example, the practice and dedication of the Tibetan monks took place over the vast majority of their many years on earth, years lived mostly in isolation. And from a realistic perspective, that is not our work. The powers and accomplishments listed in the Vibhuti Pada are for those who have moved beyond the more superficial realms of the practice of yoga and into the system's much deeper challenges.

How you do anything is how you do everything. And the more you look at what you are trying to create from the standpoint of your deepest beliefs, the more you will be able to clear up those pesky thoughts that are still holding on for dear life—and holding you back from full creativity. Just as the tiniest splinter in one toe can affect an entire foot, the smallest divergence in the subconscious mind away from lining up will keep you out of alignment.

---

47   B. K. S. Iyengar, *Light on the Yoga Sutras of Patanjali*, p. 195

So, please, stop believing in miracles. You need only believe in yourself.

The future belongs to those who believe in the beauty of their dreams.

~ Eleanor Roosevelt

For Today:

1. Continue with meditation.

2. Believe, believe, believe!

Supplemental information, support and community for vibers can be found online at www.vibeathon.com.

Remember, what you perceive you receive ... Now, vibe on!

Day Twenty-eight: Metamorphosis

I must be willing to give up what I am in order to become what I will be.

~ Albert Einstein

Does a seed know that eventually it will become a flower? Most likely, no. If a flower seed was required to endure the kinds of mental activity that we humans do, upon hearing proclamation that it will someday morph into a colorful, fragrant bloom it would most likely respond that such a thing was utter nonsense. The seed is clear in its current manifestation as a seed. It's completely wrapped up in its seedness. And so, for you to imply that it will someday move beyond its seedness to something far greater is absurd, because the seed knows of no possibility other than its present state.

The seed is planted in the perfect soil, with access to appropriate sun and water so that it is nourished in a manner suitable to and in support of it becoming more than what it presently is. As the seed opens itself to the elements that now surround and foster transformation, it begins to let go of its identification as a seed. It must, for if it doesn't fully let go of its seedness, it will never fully come into what it is meant to be. And then, not only will it never flower, it will never provide pollen for the bees, further nourishment of the soil, scent for the air, and inspiration for poets and lovers.

The seed must be willing to give up what it is in order to become what it will be. And you must be willing to do the same. For in this season of metamorphosis that has been your Vibe-a-Thon, you have moved closer to what it is you are looking to create. You have embraced the *upaya*, or method, by which to start reaching that aim. This is great, but what is far greater is the fact that while the hope was to use the means to get to the goal, in reality the *upaya* has been the process to get back to YOU. And *this* you is a brighter, clearer you, more connected with the intuitive understanding of your Soul's path—your true dharma. Like the seed becoming a flower, it's time for you to let this new you find expression out in the world.

We suffer when we try to hold on to the remnants of who we once were. And cling-ing to our former identities is not possible, because we are ever-changing beings—as affected daily by the elements as the seedling is affected by sun and rain. We are in con-stant evolution. In order to live consciously and freely within ourselves, we must rec-ognize when those previous identifications are no longer relevant to who we now are. When we take responsibility for all that we have become, we bloom. The qualities we have developed within ourselves have no possible course of action but to demonstrate themselves out in the world. And then, as the flower stands in service to the bees and the poets and the lovers, so too will the magnificent example that is you inspire those around you to become truer versions of themselves.

Let the Silence take you to the core of life.

~ Rumi

As you continue to open beyond your perception of reality and closer to that which is the truest part of you, what you experience is self-understanding, self-ac-ceptance, absolute trust and faith, and unbounded love. And when you are open to that kind of love, what you look to create *can't help but be an articulation of that love.*

We must not hold such expressions of love back from the world, because if we don't set them free how can we possibly say that we have truly created? As Oscar Hammerstein wrote in a beautiful lyric, "Love isn't love 'til you give it away."

When we send these expressions of our deepest selves out more and more, life moves beyond the mundane tasks that bring us through the hours of a day and into the deepening, graceful navigation away from contrast and toward evidence and opportunity in an ever-expanding dance of life. In the realization that creativ-ity is nothing more than the process of dancing with oneself, we no longer create as much for our own ego needs. We find that *creating in service to others* is truly, and in a very direct way, the best creating we can do. We become the change we want to see in the world, foster the greater implications of that change out in the world, and reap the benefits of the change . . . as will all beings.

And, in the end . . . the love you take is equal to the love you make.

~ John Lennon and Paul McCartney

For Today:

1. Continue with meditation.

2. For consideration: Have you truly moved into the new you that you have created? Or are there some pieces of you holding on to those remnants of the old you? If there are (and for most of us, there will be), take some time today to visualize letting go of them. Perhaps in the form of a graduation ceremony, or Post-it notes that you peel off and discard. If you find that those notes are really sticky, just stay with the work!

Supplemental information, support and community for vibers can be found online at www.vibeathon.com.

Remember, what you perceive you receive . . . Now, vibe on!

The End . . . or the Beginning

Silence is painful, but in silence things take form, and we must wait and watch. In us, in our secret depth, lies the knowing element which sees and hears that which we do not see and hear. All our percep-tions, all the things we have done, all that we are today, dwelt once in that knowing, silent depth, that treasure chamber in the soul. And we are more than we think. We are more than we know. That which is more than we think and know is always seeking and adding to itself while we are doing nothing—or think we are doing nothing. But to be conscious of what is going on in our depth is to help it along. When subconsciousness becomes consciousness, the seeds in our winter-clad-selves turn to flowers, and the silent light in us sings with all its might.

~ Kahlil Gibran

I'm writing this as I sit on the second floor of NYC's City Bakery, in my favor-ite spot—a long, barlike table that overlooks most of the restaurant. Large iced coffee to my left, pen and notebook slightly askew in front of me and a world of patrons below. It's a majestic, somewhat powerful experience up here as witness. I feel almost like the Wizard of Oz or a bird taking respite from flight.

There's a long line of people waiting to pay for their food. Most have a tray of assorted items from the food bar. Others have nothing yet, but will soon have coffee, a cookie, or a tart in their possession.

Interesting to note that no two people have made the same selections. Oh, wait . . . I see a couple. Each is receiving what looks like the same item—a choco-late chip cookie. But on second thought, it's not the same cookie, for each one is a unique creation. Each treat may have come from the same batter, but I bet you anything that on closer inspection than my bird's eye view, we would discern individuality.

Life is exactly like this flow of people. We are individual creators with unique wishes and desired manifestations. And in the same way that I might decide to go for a large iced coffee, you may prefer a helping of the macaroni and cheese (which I can smell from here and would highly recommend). You may buy a tart for dessert later on and I may opt for a dozen assorted cookies to eat right now. I may pay with exact change, while you might use a credit card. And as we walk out of the bakery with our selections in hand, we would be happy with our choices and excited at the prospect of enjoying it all.

Isn't it wonderful, amazing, fantastic to know that this is, in fact, what life is all about? That all of us, as unique individuals, are absolutely within our right to create the lives that we desire and to do so from a place of great pleasure in knowing that creating comes from within—from the very core of the Soul. And all those around us have the same right—to figure out, from their place of peace inside, what it is that they would like to offer as their expression.

Isn't it great to know that we are meant to live in joy and abundance, in a state of constant evolution where things are meant only to get better and better and better?

You are at the end of your monthlong Vibe-a-Thon, and (I hope) at the beginning of a new way of life. For everything that you have learned in this past month, as you focused on your chosen subject, can and should be applied not only to creating individual things, but to creating your life in its entirety.

A fellow viber came to a yoga class that I was teaching during a previous Vibe-a-Thon. Before class, she informed me that she felt she was on the brink of a cold and would therefore take it easy during the class . . . she had holidays coming up and was afraid of becoming sick and missing them. When I asked her if she had taken any time to vibe on feeling good and having a great, healthy holiday, she looked at me as though it were a completely foreign concept! But a second later the light bulb came on.

"Oh yeah . . . I didn't think of that!" she said.

I advised her to take it easy, but to hold the vision of wellness—and fun holidays—during the class. By the middle of class, she was kicking up into handstand with as much gusto as the rest of the practitioners.

At the end of class, she came up to me with a beaming smile. "Thank you!" she said. "I feel completely fine now . . . actually, I feel great!"

"I'm glad you feel better," I replied. "But don't thank me. I did nothing—you simply created your own reality."

We do create our own reality, for all reality is perceived. And once you really begin to understand that, the world becomes your playground. You have health. You have love. You have security in all its many forms.

You have fulfillment. And the more you do this work—the more you live consciously—the more you will find that not only can you have or be or do anything you want, but that you don't really need as much as you may have thought. Because the peace you feel inside is truly the source of all fulfillment.

You set your intention and line up vibrationally with that which you desire. Through the process of meditation, you learn how to come away from the distracting thoughts and the field of your previously limited perception begins to open, as you move beyond the ego self and closer to the true Self. You take that greater sense of clarity and ease from meditation and apply it to staying mindful in your daily life—understanding that reactions that keep us from staying in a good place on the vibrational spectrum stem from previous conditioning and experiences, and that it is now your work to lessen their effect on you. As you continue the work, you redefine your actions based on the contrast and collect evidence that you are moving on the right path. You take the opportunities that present themselves by staying in an open state of curiosity and avoiding the tendency toward judgment. And when you feel yourself wavering off the path of what you desire, you use the Vibrational Emergency Management Kit to help you get back on track.

This is creating through the path of yoga. This path is that of Oneness, and in coming to a place within where there is only truth, love, and abundance, we reconcile the disparate parts. As when all parts of an engine are working smoothly, when we are in a cohesive, unified experience of our internal Self, that clarity and unwavering confidence will surely steer us in the right direction.

You have the keys to the kingdom. And the only limitations you have in what you can create are *those limitations you impose on yourself*. Because the tools for creating are the same for everything—there's no difference between creating a thimble or a castle!

> *Gradually, one's mastery in concentration extends from the smallest particle to the greatest magnitude. (Sutra 1.40)*

And so, it begs the question:

What do you want? What do you really, really want your life to be?

I am sitting here on my perch at City Bakery. I teach yoga and am now the author of a book on how to manifest through yoga philosophy, meditation, and mindfulness. This is my creation, born from a place deep inside that sought to understand how designing one's life fit with these practices, a search that led to a desire to serve others by sharing my explorations with those who might benefit from them.

Years ago, I was a marketing associate at a private equity firm, having just handed in my resignation and nothing shy of petrified at the prospect of my future. When I made the decision to follow this path, there was uncertainty. It was a new, *very ambiguous* road for someone who comes from a long line of wonderful people who have made—and continue to make—their way in more established careers. And so, when my dad responded to the news of my resignation with "Well J., the die has been cast . . ." (in the perfect, gently ominous tone of a retired banker trying to come to terms with his free-spirited daughter's plunge-taking), it took some time to get my vibe going. But I used the tools. I did the work. I held my vision and continue to line up with it. It's a never-ending process, this creating a life. But you know what? Pops was right. The die was cast. And the returns on the throw of that die are far greater than anything I ever could have imagined. No more bad or good, now there is only contrast, evidence, and opportunity, helping me make my way forward in this never-ending process that is the dance of the creative life.

My heartfelt hope is that the path unfolds for you in a way that is filled with joy and adventure. And I wish you an abundance of health, peace, and happiness as you continue to create the magnificence that is you.

Exercises for Keeping the Vibe Going

Exercise #1: Where are you in regards to the subject of your Vibe-a-Thon?

Where are you with regards to the subject of your Vibe-a-Thon? Has it manifested for you, or are you still on the path toward manifestation?

If you are still on the path, continue to work with the tools and hold your vision. Repeat the process of the Vibe-a-Thon as many times as you need to and know that some things take longer than others, depending on the strength of your vibe and the potency of the disallowing beliefs. So stick with it!

If you have manifested the subject of your Vibe-a-Thon, take a moment to congratulate yourself. A pat on the back well deserved.

Exercise #2: What have you learned during the Vibe-a-Thon?

Take a few moments to appreciate the new ways of thinking you have incorporated into your mental landscape. Not only is it great to acknowledge, but it's also a way of making those things a bit more concrete . . . for future use!

Exercise #3: What do you really want?

Begin dialoguing with yourself about the way you would like your life to play out. We start by taking the examples of the smaller "things" we work to manifest, but the big picture is just as easy to create using the tools you've learned. Start formulating your vision . . . then line up and see what happens!

And ALWAYS remember, what you perceive you receive . . . Vibe on, vibe on, vibe on!

With Gratitude

The Vibe-a-Thon has been ten years in the making. While it would be impossible for me to list all of those who have been a part of this journey – providing both evidence and contrast leading to this point – I give loving thanks to the following:

To Jennie Cohen, my copyeditor, who approached the manuscript with enthusiasm, sensitivity and great respect for this work. Thank you, Jennie, for making the words sparkle more brightly.

To Mariellen Carpentieri, photographer extraordinaire. My gratitude for the wonderful photo on the back cover is surpassed by the joy of reconnecting after so many years. Thank you, dear friend.

To Abigail Russell, aka She Who Glides on Water of Tribe Vibe. Thank you for your beautiful work on the cover of this book. Both them, and you, are lovely beyond description.

To the community of teachers at Yoga Works, especially Chrissy Carter, Jenny Aurthur, Jodie Rufty and Paula Lynch. The business that we are in can be competitive and - let's just say it - quite egocentric. Your open-minded support, love, and sidesplitting humor are gifts that I hope to treasure for years to come.

To all of the students, trainees and mentees who I have had the privilege to serve, thank you. What I have been able to share with you is miniscule in comparison to what you continue to teach me.

To Katy Roemer and Pamela Steigmeyer… the friendship that I have received from you over the years is a profound gift and I am forever grateful for it.

To my mentor and friend, Ginny Duffy. Thank you for guiding me and seeing the possibilities when I was not able to. My gratitude to you is unmeasured.

It is evident from the book that I come from a large, close-knit family. Quite simply, I am who I am because of them – Paolillo, Brown, Illes, Gallant, Wall, Scicutella, and the community of family friends that surrounded and nurtured me. My love and thanks to all of you, for never requiring me to be anything other than myself - and for witnessing my path from a place of curiosity and not judgment.

And always, for Jack and Wilma - the two furry creatures that taught me what this is all about.

Jeanmarie Paolillo is a teacher, teacher trainer and mentor at Yoga Works in New York City. She leads trainings and workshops on asana, the philosophy of yoga, meditation and mindfulness, and the energetic body internationally. The fundamental purpose of yoga for Jeanmarie is learning to be present in the moment. She lives in the passionate belief that all things in life are possible and that manifestation requires an understanding that everything is the culmination of our thoughts. The journey of yoga leads the practitioner to a place of awareness regarding the life they are creating so they can consciously create their lives - as evidenced by her own leap from the corporate world after 20 years. Jeanmarie has been featured in Natural Health Magazine, Cosmopolitan, Yoga Journal and has appeared on Weddings.com and the CBS Morning Show. She is part of the Expert Network for Greatest.com and a featured contributor to The Daily Love. She holds a B.A. in Psychology from Indiana University and has completed studies toward a Certificate in Applied Positive Psychology (May, 2013). The Vibe-a-Thon is her first book.

Bibliography

Barks, Coleman, Reynold Nicholson, A. J. Arberry, and John Moyne, trans. *The Essential Rumi*. San Francisco: HarperSanFrancisco, 2004.

Benson, Herbert, and Miriam Klipper. *The Relaxation Response*. New York: HarperCollins, 1975.

Benson, Herbert, and William Proctor. *Beyond the Relaxation Response*. New York: Berkley Books, 1984.

Bolte Taylor, Jill. *My Stroke of Insight*. New York: Viking Penguin, 2008.

Carrera, Rev. Jaganath. *Inside the Yoga Sutras*. Buckingham, Va.: Integral Yoga Publications, 2006.

Desikachar, T. K. V. *The Heart of Yoga*. Rochester, Vt.: Inner Traditions International, 1995.

Doidge, Norman. *The Brain That Changes Itself*. New York: Viking Penguin, 2007.

Easwaran, Eknath. *The Bhagavad Gita*. Boston: Shambhala Publications, 2004.

—*The Upanishads*. Berkeley: Nilgiri Press, 1987.

Emerson, Ralph Waldo. *The Essential Writings of Ralph Waldo Emerson*. Ed. Brooks Atkinson. New York: Random House, 2000.

Emoto, Masaru. *The Hidden Messages in Water*. Hillsboro, Ore.: Beyond Words Publishing, 2004.

Frawley, David. *Yoga and Ayurveda*. Twin Lakes, Wis.: Lotus Press, 1999.

Fredrickson, Barbara. *Positivity*. New York: Crown Publishers, 2009.

Goswami, Amit. *How Quantum Activism Can Save Civilization*. Charlottesville, Va.: Hampton Roads Publishing Company, 2011.

Hanson, Rick, and Richard Mendius. *Buddha's Brain*. Oakland, Calif.: New Harbinger Publications, 2009.

Iyengar, B. K. S. *Light on the Yoga Sutras of Patanjali*.: HarperCollins Publishers India, 1993.

— *The Tree of Yoga*. Boston: Shambhala Classics, 2002.

Judith, Anodea. *Eastern Body, Western Mind*. Berkeley: Celestial Arts Publishing, 1996.

Lad, Vasant. *Textbook of Ayurveda: A Complete Guide to Clinical Assessment*. Albuquerque: The Ayurvedic Press, 2006.

Ladinsky, Daniel, trans. *The Gift: Poems by Hafiz, The Great Sufi Master*. New York: Penguin Compass, 1999.

Lipton, Bruce. *The Biology of Belief*. Carlsbad, Calif.: Hay House, Inc., 2005.

Mitchell, Stephen. *Bhagavad Gita*. New York: Three Rivers Press, 2000.

Satchidananda, Sri Swami. *The Yoga Sutras of Pantanjali*. Yogaville, Va.: Integral Yoga Publications, 1978.

Index